Contents

3

Ninja Air Fryer

Cookbook for Beginners

1000-Day Healthier, Easier, & Crispier Air Fryer Recipes Using European Measurements

Isobel Miles

Ninja Air Fryer Series comes with another interesting and exciting new addition- the Ninja Max XL Air Fryer. This model is not only capable of air frying, but it can give the food some added crispiness as well. Unlike other air fryers, this model provides a Max Crisp mode along with the air roasting, air broiling, baking, air frying, dehydrating and reheating options. In this cookbook, we shall discover all the different ways to use this air fryer and how you can handle it during cooking and after it. So let's get started!

What is Ninja Max XL Air Fryer?

The Ninja Max XL Air Fryer is a convenient and quick way to prepare your favorite foods. In a family-sized 5.5-quart basket, cook and crisp 3 pounds of French fries with little to no oil. Maxcrisp technology uses 450°F superheated air to cook dishes up to 30 per cent faster (compared to Ninja AF100), resulting in hotter, crispier results with little to no oil for guilt-free fried favorites. The Ninja Max XL Air Fryer has revolutionized kitchen technology to the point where users can now enjoy fresh, crispy food in no time. The control panel is present on top of the basket's inlets and covers the air fryer's front top part. The air fryer's top is flat, and it does not emit a lot of heat. However, nothing should be placed on the flat top of the air fryer machine or anywhere near it. The control panel features function and operation buttons. The following are the other function and operation keys.

Function Buttons of Ninja Max XL Air Fryer

The function buttons present on the control panel are there to select the desired mode of cooking. Here are the options that you can see on the Ninja Max XL Air Fryer:

• **Max Crisp:** It is an advanced mode that can add extra crispiness to the food through high temperatures and enhance air flow without using any oil.
• **Air Fry:** This option lets you air fry any food.
• **Air Roast:** The option also gets you to meats, poultry, seafood, vegetables and more.
• **Air Broil:** This option lets you add caramelized color on top of the food.
• **Bake:** The bake mode will allow you to bake cookies, cakes, or other desserts and baked treats.
• **Reheat:** Using this mode; you can easily reheat the already cooked food.
• **Dehydrate:** With this option, you can dehydrate fruits, meats, and vegetables at extremely low temperatures.

Operating Buttons of Ninja Max XL Air Fryer

The control panel also has some added keys which allow you to adjust the time and temperature. Here is how you can use these buttons:

TEMP arrows: These arrow keys are present on the control, which lets you adjust the temperature of a specific cooking mode. The up and down keys can be used to decrease and increase the temperature.

TIME arrows: You can adjust the cooking time using the up and down time keys.

START/STOP button: Once you have selected the desired cooking mode, time and temperature, you can press the START/STOP button to initiate cooking.

POWER button: The power button is there switch on the appliance.

The control panel has a screen that displays the time in hours and minutes. The same screen also shows the set temperature of the air fryer.

Cooking Tips

Cleaning and maintenance are also two important steps to keep the appliance working and running. Here are a few easy and simple tips that will help you get good results every time:

- Set the ingredients in a uniform layer on the bottom of the basket with no overlapping for consistent browning. If your ingredients are overlapping, give them a good shake halfway through the cooking period.
- Cooking time and temperature can be changed at any point during the process. To change the time or temperature, simply push the up and down TIME or TEMP arrows.
- Reduce the temperature of the air fryer by 25 degrees F to convert recipes from a regular oven. To avoid overcooking, check your meal periodically.

The recommended preheating time is 3 minutes. A 3-minute countdown can be set using the built-in timer. If you are not preheating the appliance, then you add this preheating time to the total cooking time of the appliance.

The crisper plate lifts the ingredients in the basket, allowing air to circulate beneath and around them for crisp, uniform results. After selecting a cooking function, push the START/STOP button to begin cooking right away. The thermostat and timer will be set to the default settings.

Get Started with the Ninja Max XL Air Fryer

If you are new to the Ninja Max XL Air Fryer and don't know how to operate it well, then here are a few simple tips to get started.

1. First, unbox the appliance and carefully place it on a flat and stable surface.
2. Check all the components of the appliance and plug it in.
3. Set the crisper plate in the air fryer basket first.
4. Select the mode as desired-Max Crisp/Air Fry/Air Roast/Bake/Air Broil/Dehydrate function.
5. To set the cooking time, use the TIME up and down arrow buttons.
6. Fill the basket with ingredients. Place the basket inside the unit. To begin cooking, press START/STOP.
7. Remove its basket from the air fryer and shake it back and forth to toss the ingredients during cooking. When the basket is removed, the unit will automatically pause. Cooking will resume once the basket is reinserted.
8. So, when cooking is finished, the unit will beep, and "End" will show on the control panel.
9. Remove out the ingredients or use oven mitts or silicone-tipped tongs/utensils to remove them.

Brussels Sprouts Potato Hash

Prep Time: 15 minutes.

Cook Time: 10 minutes.

Serves: 4

Ingredients:

- 2 cups Brussels sprouts
- 1 small to medium red onion
- 2 cups baby red potatoes
- 2 tablespoons avocado oil
- ½ teaspoons salt
- ½ teaspoons black pepper

Preparation:

1. Peel and boil potatoes in salted water in a suitable pot for 15 minutes until soft.

2. Drain and allow them to cool down then dice.

3. Shred Brussels sprouts and toss them with potatoes and the rest of the ingredients.

4. Divide this veggies hash mixture in the air fryer basket.

5. Return the air fryer basket to the Ninja Max XL Air Fryer.

6. Choose the "Max Crisp" mode with 375 degrees F temperature and 10 minutes of cooking time.

7. Initiate cooking by pressing the START/STOP BUTTON.

8. Shake the veggies once cooked halfway through.

9. Serve warm.

Serving Suggestion: Serve the potato hash with toasted bread slices

Variation Tip: Broccoli or cauliflower florets can also be used instead of Brussel sprouts

Nutritional Information Per Serving:

Calories 305 | Fat 25g |Sodium 532mg | Carbs 2.3g | Fiber 0.4g | Sugar 2g | Protein 18.3g

Jelly Doughnuts

Prep Time: 10 minutes.

Cook Time: 6 minutes.

Serves: 4

Ingredients:

- 1 package Pillsbury Grands
- ½ cup seedless raspberry jelly
- 1 tablespoon butter, melted
- ½ cup sugar

Preparation:

1. Spread the Pillsbury dough and cut out 3 inches round doughnuts out of it.
2. Place the doughnuts in the air fryer basket and brush them with butter.
3. Drizzle sugar over the doughnuts.
4. Return the air fryer basket to the Ninja Max XL Air Fryer.
5. Choose the "Max Crisp" mode at 320 degrees F and 6 minutes of cooking time.
6. Initiate cooking by pressing the START/STOP BUTTON.
7. Use a piping bag to inject raspberry jelly into each doughnut.
8. Serve.

Serving Suggestion: Serve the doughnuts with strawberry compote

Variation Tip: Drizzle shredded coconut on top

Nutritional Information Per Serving:
Calories 102 | Fat 7.6g |Sodium 545mg | Carbs 1.5g | Fiber 0.4g | Sugar 0.7g | Protein 7.1g

Cheesy Baked Eggs

Prep Time: 10 minutes.

Cook Time: 16 minutes.

Serves: 4

Ingredients:

- 4 large eggs
- 57g smoked gouda, shredded
- Everything bagel seasoning, to taste
- Salt and pepper to taste

Preparation:

1. Crack one egg in each ramekin.
2. Top the egg with bagel seasoning, black pepper, salt and gouda.
3. Place 2 ramekins in the air fryer basket.
4. Return the air fryer basket to the Ninja Max XL Air Fryer.
5. Choose the "Air Fry" mode and set the temperature to 400 degrees F and 16 minutes of cooking time.
6. Initiate cooking by pressing the START/STOP BUTTON.
7. Serve warm.

Serving Suggestion: Serve the eggs with toasted bread slices and crispy bacon

Variation Tip: Add herbed cream on top of the eggs

Nutritional Information Per Serving:

Calories 190 | Fat 18g |Sodium 150mg | Carbs 0.6g | Fiber 0.4g | Sugar 0.4g | Protein 7.2g

Apple Fritters

Prep Time: 15 minutes.
Cook Time: 7 minutes.
Serves: 4

Ingredients:

- 2 apples, cored and diced
- 1 cup all-purpose flour
- 2 tablespoons sugar
- 1 teaspoon baking powder
- ½ teaspoons salt
- ½ teaspoons ground cinnamon
- ¼ teaspoon ground nutmeg
- 79 ml milk
- 2 tablespoons butter, melted
- 1 egg
- ½ teaspoons lemon juice

Cinnamon Glaze

- ½ cup confectioners' sugar
- 2 tablespoons milk
- ½ teaspoons ground cinnamon
- Pinch of salt

Preparation:

1. Mix flour, sugar and the rest of the batter ingredients in a suitable bowl until smooth.
2. Fold in apples and mix evenly.
3. Layer the air fryer basket with parchment paper.
4. Drop the batter spoon by spoon into the basket with a 1-inch gap between each fritter.
5. Return the air fryer basket to the Ninja Max XL Air Fryer.
6. Choose the "Max Crisp" mode at 370 degrees F and 7 minutes of cooking time.
7. Initiate cooking by pressing the START/STOP BUTTON.
8. Meanwhile, mix salt, cinnamon, milk, and sugar in a suitable bowl.
9. Serve the crispy fritters with the glaze on top.

Serving Suggestion: Serve the fritters with your favorite cream dip

Variation Tip: Add chopped nuts to the batter

Nutritional Information Per Serving:

Calories 282 | Fat 15g |Sodium 526mg | Carbs 20g | Fiber 0.6g | Sugar 3.3g | Protein 16g

Breakfast Potatoes

Prep Time: 15 minutes.

Cook Time: 20 minutes.

Serves: 6

Ingredients:

- 3 potatoes, peeled and diced
- 1 onion yellow, diced
- 1 green pepper diced
- 2 teaspoons salt
- ½ teaspoons pepper
- 2 tablespoons olive oil
- 1 cup cheese shredded

Preparation:

1. Toss potatoes with onion, green peppers, black pepper, salt and cheese in a suitable bowl.

2. Add the potato mixture into the Ninja Air fryer basket.

3. Return the air fryer basket to the Ninja Max XL Air Fryer.

4. Choose the "Air Fry" mode at 400 degrees F temperature and 20 minutes of cooking time.

5. Initiate cooking by pressing the START/STOP BUTTON.

6. Toss the veggies once cooked halfway through.

7. Serve warm.

Serving Suggestion: Serve the potatoes with bread

Variation Tip: Add crumbled bacon to the

Nutritional Information Per Serving:
Calories 209 | Fat 7.5g |Sodium 321mg | Carbs 34.1g | Fiber 4g | Sugar 3.8g | Protein 4.3g

Cornbread

Prep Time: 15 minutes.

Cook Time: 15 minutes.

Serves: 6

Ingredients:

- 1 cup cornmeal
- 1 cup all-purpose flour
- 1 tablespoon sugar
- 2 teaspoons baking powder
- ½ teaspoons baking soda
- ½ teaspoons salt
- 1 stick butter melted
- 1½ cups buttermilk
- 2 eggs
- 113g diced chiles

Preparation:

1. Mix cornmeal with flour, sugar, baking powder, baking soda, salt, butter, milk, eggs and chiles in a suitable bowl until smooth.
2. Spread this mixture in greased 8-inch baking pan.
3. Place pan in the air fryer basket.
4. Return the air fryer basket to the Ninja Max XL Air Fryer.
5. Choose the "Max Crisp" mode at 330 degrees F and 15 minutes of cooking time.
6. Initiate cooking by pressing the START/STOP BUTTON.
7. Slice and serve.

Serving Suggestion: Serve the bread with chocolate syrup or Nutella spread

Variation Tip: Use almond flour instead of all-purpose flour

Nutritional Information Per Serving:

Calories 199 | Fat 11.1g |Sodium 297mg |

Carbs 14.9g | Fiber 1g | Sugar 2.5g | Protein 9.9g

Breakfast Stuffed Peppers

Prep Time: 10 minutes.

Cook Time: 13 minutes.

Serves: 4

Ingredients:

- 2 capsicums, halved, seeds removed
- 4 eggs
- 1 teaspoon olive oil
- 1 pinch salt and pepper
- 1 pinch sriracha flakes

Preparation:

1. Cut each capsicum in half and place the halves in the air fryer basket.
2. Crack one egg into each capsicum and top it with black pepper, salt, sriracha flakes and olive oil.
3. Return the air fryer basket to the Ninja Max XL Air Fryer.

4. Choose the "Air Fry" mode at 390 degrees F and 13 minutes of cooking time.

5. Initiate cooking by pressing the START/STOP BUTTON.

6. Serve warm.

Serving Suggestion: Serve the peppers with toasted bread slices and crispy bacon

Variation Tip: Sprinkle dried herbs on top before serving

Nutritional Information Per Serving:
Calories 237 | Fat 19g |Sodium 518mg | Carbs 7g | Fiber 1.5g | Sugar 3.4g | Protein 12g

Roasted Oranges

Prep Time: 15 minutes.

Cook Time: 6 minutes.

Serves: 4

Ingredients:

- 2 oranges, halved
- 2 teaspoons honey
- 1 teaspoon cinnamon

Preparation:

1. Place the oranges in the air fryer basket.

2. Drizzle honey and cinnamon over the orange halves.

3. Return the air fryer basket to the Ninja Max XL Air Fryer.

4. Choose the "Air Fry" mode at 395 degrees F temperature and 6 minutes of cooking time.

5. Initiate cooking by pressing the START/STOP BUTTON.

6. Serve.

Serving Suggestion: Serve the oranges with baked muffins

Variation Tip: Use maple syrup instead of honey

Nutritional Information Per Serving:
Calories 183 | Fat 15g |Sodium 402mg | Carbs 2.5g | Fiber 0.4g | Sugar 1.1g | Protein 10g

Sausage Breakfast Casserole

Prep Time: 10 minutes.

Cook Time: 10 minutes.

Serves: 4

Ingredients:

- 453.5g hash browns
- 453.5g ground breakfast sausage
- 1 green capsicum diced
- 1 red capsicum diced
- 1 yellow capsicum diced
- ¼ cup sweet onion diced
- 4 eggs

Preparation:

1. Layer the air fryer basket with parchment paper.
2. Place the hash browns in the basket.
3. Spread sausage, onion and peppers over the hash brown.
4. Return the air fryer basket to the Ninja Max XL Air Fryer.
5. Choose the "Max Crisp" mode at 355 degrees F temperature and 10 minutes of cooking time.
6. Initiate cooking by pressing the START/STOP BUTTON.
7. Beat 4 eggs in a suitable bowl and pour over the air fried veggies.
8. Continue air frying for 10 minutes..
9. Garnish with salt and black pepper.
10. Serve warm.

Serving Suggestion: Serve the casserole with toasted bread and eggs

Variation Tip: Add black pepper and salt for seasoning

Nutritional Information Per Serving:
Calories 267 | Fat 12g |Sodium 165mg | Carbs 39g | Fiber 1.4g | Sugar 22g | Protein 3.3g

Breakfast Frittata

Prep Time: 10 minutes.

Cook Time: 12 minutes.

Serves: 4

Ingredients:

- 4 eggs
- 4 tablespoons milk
- 35g cheddar cheese grated
- 50g feta crumbled
- 1 tomato, deseeded and chopped
- 15g spinach chopped
- 1 tablespoon fresh herbs, chopped
- 2 spring onion chopped
- Salt and black pepper, to taste
- ½ teaspoon olive oil

Preparation:

1. Beat eggs with milk in a suitable bowl and stir in the rest of the ingredients.

2. Grease a suitable pan and line with parchment paper.

3. Add the egg mixture into the pan and place in the air fryer basket.

4. Return the air fryer basket to the Ninja Max XL Air Fryer.

5. Choose the "Air Fry" mode at 350 degrees F and 12 minutes of cooking time.

6. Initiate cooking by pressing the START/STOP BUTTON.

7. Serve warm.

Serving Suggestion: Serve the frittata bread slices

Variation Tip: Add salt and black pepper for seasoning.

Nutritional Information Per Serving:

Calories 273 | Fat 22g |Sodium 517mg | Carbs 3.3g | Fiber 0.2g | Sugar 1.4g | Protein 16.1g

Fried Cheese

Prep Time: 10 minutes.

Cook Time: 12 minutes.

Serves: 4

Ingredients:

- 1 Mozzarella cheese block, cut into sticks
- 2 teaspoons olive oil

Preparation:

1. Add the cheese slices into the Ninja Air fryer basket.

2. Drizzle olive oil over the cheese slices.

3. Return the air fryer basket to the Ninja Max XL Air Fryer.

4. Choose the "Max Crisp" mode and set the temperature to 360 degrees F and 12 minutes of cooking time.

5. Flip the cheese slices once cooked halfway through.

6. Serve.

Serving Suggestion: Serve with fresh yogurt dip or cucumber salad

Variation Tip: Add black pepper and salt for seasoning

Nutritional Information Per Serving:

Calories 186 | Fat 3g |Sodium 223mg | Carbs 31g | Fiber 8.7g | Sugar 5.5g | Protein 9.7g

Avocado Fries With Sriracha Dip

Prep Time: 10 minutes.

Cook Time: 6 minutes.

Serves: 4

Ingredients:

Avocado Fries

- 4 avocados, peeled and cut into sticks
- ¾ cup panko breadcrumbs

- ¼ cup flour
- 2 eggs, beaten
- ½ teaspoons garlic powder
- ½ teaspoons salt

Sriracha-Ranch Sauce

- ¼ cup ranch dressing
- 1 teaspoon sriracha sauce

Preparation:

1. Mix flour with garlic powder and salt in a suitable bowl.
2. Dredge the avocado sticks through the flour mixture.
3. Dip them in the eggs and coat them with breadcrumbs.
4. Place the coated fries in the air fryer basket.
5. Return the air fryer basket to the Ninja Max XL Air Fryer.
6. Choose the "Air Fry" mode at 400 degrees F and 6 minutes of cooking time.
7. Initiate cooking by pressing the START/STOP BUTTON.
8. Flip the fries once cooked halfway through.
9. Mix all the sriracha dipping sauce ingredients in a suitable bowl.
10. Serve the fries with dipping sauce.

Serving Suggestion: Serve with tomato sauce or cream cheese dip

Variation Tip: Use crushed cornflakes for breading to have extra crispiness

Nutritional Information Per Serving:
Calories 229 | Fat 1.9 |Sodium 567mg | Carbs 1.9g | Fiber 0.4g | Sugar 0.6g | Protein 11.8g

Fried Ravioli

Prep Time: 15 minutes.
Cook Time: 7 minutes.
Serves: 6

Ingredients:

- 12 frozen raviolis
- 118ml buttermilk
- ½ cup Italian breadcrumbs

Preparation:

1. Dip the ravioli in the buttermilk then coat with the breadcrumbs.
2. Add the ravioli into the Ninja Air fryer basket.
3. Return the air fryer basket to the Ninja Max XL Air Fryer.

4. Choose the "Air Fry" mode and set the temperature to 400 degrees F and 7 minutes of cooking time.

5. Initiate cooking by pressing the START/STOP BUTTON.

6. Flip the ravioli once cooked halfway through.

7. Serve warm.

Serving Suggestion: Serve with tomato or sweet chili sauce

Variation Tip: Use crushed cornflakes for breading to have extra crispiness

Nutritional Information Per Serving:

Calories 134 | Fat 5.9g |Sodium 343mg | Carbs 9.5g | Fiber 0.5g | Sugar 1.1g | Protein 10.4g

Mozzarella Balls

Prep Time: 10 minutes.

Cook Time: 13 minutes.

Serves: 6

Ingredients:

- 2 cups mozzarella, shredded
- 3 tablespoons cornstarch
- 3 tablespoons water
- 2 eggs, beaten
- 1 cup Italian seasoned breadcrumbs
- 1 tablespoon Italian seasoning
- 1½ teaspoons garlic powder
- 1 teaspoon salt
- 1½ teaspoons Parmesan

Preparation:

1. Mix mozzarella with parmesan, water and cornstarch in a suitable bowl.

2. Make 1-inch balls out of this mixture.

3. Mix breadcrumbs with seasoning, salt, and garlic powder in a suitable bowl.

4. Dip the balls into the beaten eggs and coat with the breadcrumbs.

5. Place the coated balls in the air fryer basket.

6. Return the air fryer basket to the Ninja Max XL Air Fryer.

7. Choose the "Air Fry" mode and set the temperature to 360 degrees F and 13 minutes of cooking time.

8. Initiate cooking by pressing the START/STOP BUTTON.

9. Toss the balls once cooked halfway through.

10. Serve.

Serving Suggestion: Serve with tomato ketchup, Asian coleslaw, or creamed cabbage

Variation Tip: Toss fried balls with black pepper for a change of taste

Nutritional Information Per Serving:

Calories 307 | Fat 8.6g | Sodium 510mg | Carbs 22.2g | Fiber 1.4g | Sugar 13g | Protein 33.6g

Bacon Wrapped Tater Tots

Prep Time: 10 minutes.

Cook Time: 14 minutes.

Serves: 8

Ingredients:

- 8 bacon slices
- 3 tablespoons honey
- ½ tablespoon chipotle chile powder
- 16 frozen tater tots

Preparation:

1. Cut the 8 bacon slices in half and wrap each tater tot with a bacon slice.
2. Brush the bacon with honey and drizzle chipotle chile powder over them.
3. Insert a toothpick to seal the bacon.
4. Place the wrapped tots in the air fryer basket.
5. Return the air fryer basket to the Ninja Max XL Air Fryer.
6. Choose the "Air Fry" mode at 350 degrees F and 14 minutes of cooking time.
7. Initiate cooking by pressing the START/STOP BUTTON.
8. Serve warm.

Serving Suggestion: Serve with tomato sauce or cream cheese dip

Variation Tip: Brush the bacon wraps with maple syrup before cooking

Nutritional Information Per Serving:

Calories 100 | Fat 2g | Sodium 480mg | Carbs 4g | Fiber 2g | Sugar 0g | Protein 18g

Crispy Popcorn Shrimp

Prep Time: 15 minutes.

Cook Time: 6 minutes.

Serves: 4

Ingredients:

- 170g shrimp, peeled and diced
- ½ cup breadcrumbs
- Salt and black pepper to taste

- 2 eggs, beaten

Preparation:

1. Mix breadcrumbs with black pepper and salt in a suitable bowl.
2. Dip the shrimp pieces in the eggs and coat each with breadcrumbs.
3. Add the shrimp popcorn into the Air fryer basket.
4. Return the air fryer basket to the Ninja Max XL Air Fryer.
5. Choose the "Air Fry" mode at 400 degrees F and 6 minutes of cooking time.
6. Initiate cooking by pressing the START/STOP BUTTON.
7. Serve warm.

Serving Suggestion: Serve with mayonnaise or cream cheese dip

Variation Tip: Use crushed cornflakes for breading to have extra crispiness

Nutritional Information Per Serving:
Calories 180 | Fat 3.2g |Sodium 133mg | Carbs 32g | Fiber 1.1g | Sugar 1.8g | Protein 9g

Onion Rings

Prep Time: 10 minutes.
Cook Time: 7 minutes.
Serves: 4

Ingredients:

- 170g onion, sliced into rings
- ½ cup breadcrumbs
- 2 eggs, beaten
- ½ cup flour
- Salt and black pepper to taste

Preparation:

1. Mix flour, black pepper and salt in a suitable bowl.
2. Dredge the onion rings through the flour mixture.
3. Dip them in the eggs and coat with the breadcrumbs.
4. Place the coated onion rings in the air fryer basket.
5. Return the air fryer basket to the Ninja Max XL Air Fryer.
6. Choose the "Max Crisp" mode at 350 degrees F and 7 minutes of cooking time.
7. Initiate cooking by pressing the START/STOP BUTTON.
8. Shake the rings once cooked halfway through.
9. Serve warm.

Serving Suggestion: Serve with ketchup, mayonnaise, or cream cheese dip

Variation Tip: Use crushed cornflakes for breading to have extra crispiness

Nutritional Information Per Serving:
Calories 185 | Fat 11g |Sodium 355mg |

Carbs 21g | Fiber 5.8g | Sugar 3g | Protein 4.7g

Potato Chips

Prep Time: 15 minutes.

Cook Time: 16 minutes.

Serves: 4

Ingredients:

- 2 large potatoes, peeled and sliced
- 1½ teaspoons salt
- 1½ teaspoons black pepper
- Oil for misting

Preparation:

1. Soak peeled and sliced potatoes in cold water for 30 minutes. then drain.
2. Pat dry the potato slices and toss them with cracked pepper, salt and oil mist.
3. Spread the potatoes in the air fryer basket.
4. Return the air fryer basket to the Ninja Max XL Air Fryer.
5. Choose the "Air Fry" mode at 300 degrees F and 16 minutes of cooking time.

6. Initiate cooking by pressing the START/STOP BUTTON.
7. Toss the fries once cooked halfway through.
8. Serve warm.

Serving Suggestion: Serve with cream cheese dip and celery sticks

Variation Tip: Use black pepper to season the chips

Nutritional Information Per Serving:
Calories 122 | Fat 1.8g |Sodium 794mg | Carbs 17g | Fiber 8.9g | Sugar 1.6g | Protein 14.9g

Cinnamon Sugar Chickpeas

Prep Time: 15 minutes.
Cook Time: 15 minutes.
Serves: 4

Ingredients:

- 2 cups chickpeas, drained
- Spray oil
- 1 tablespoon coconut sugar
- ½ teaspoons cinnamon

Serving

- 57g cheddar cheese, cubed
- ¼ cup raw almonds
- 85g jerky, sliced

Preparation:

1. Toss chickpeas with coconut sugar, cinnamon and oil in a suitable bowl.
2. Add the chickpeas into the Ninja Air fryer basket.
3. Drizzle cheddar cheese, almonds and jerky on top.
4. Return the air fryer basket to the Ninja Max XL Air Fryer.
5. Choose the "Air Fry" mode at 380 degrees F and 15 minutes of cooking time.
6. Initiate cooking by pressing the START/STOP BUTTON.
7. Toss the chickpeas once cooked halfway through.
8. Serve warm.

Serving Suggestion: Serve with guacamole, mayonnaise, or cream cheese dip

Variation Tip: Drizzle parmesan cheese on top before air frying

Nutritional Information Per Serving:
Calories 103 | Fat 8.4g |Sodium 117mg | Carbs 3.5g | Fiber 0.9g | Sugar 1.5g | Protein 5.1g

Crab Cakes

Prep Time: 10 minutes.
Cook Time: 10 minutes.
Serves: 4

Ingredients:

- 227g lump crab meat
- 1 red capsicum, chopped
- 3 green onions, chopped
- 3 tablespoons mayonnaise
- 3 tablespoons breadcrumbs
- 2 teaspoons old bay seasoning
- 1 teaspoon lemon juice

Preparation:

1. Mix crab meat with capsicum, onions and the rest of the ingredients in a food processor.
2. Make 4 inch crab cakes out of this mixture.
3. Add the crab cakes into the Ninja Air fryer basket.
4. Return the air fryer basket to the Ninja Max XL Air Fryer.
5. Choose the "Air Fry" mode at 370 degrees F and 10 minutes of cooking time.
6. Initiate cooking by pressing the START/STOP BUTTON.
7. Flip the crab cakes once cooked halfway through.
8. Serve warm.

Serving Suggestion: Serve with mayonnaise or cream cheese dip

Variation Tip: Use panko crumbs for breading to have extra crispiness

Nutritional Information Per Serving:
Calories 163 | Fat 11.5g |Sodium 918mg | Carbs 8.3g | Fiber 4.2g | Sugar 0.2g | Protein 7.4g

Chickpea Fritters

Prep Time: 10 minutes.

Cook Time: 6 minutes.

Serves: 6

Ingredients:

- 237ml plain yogurt
- 2 tablespoons sugar
- 1 tablespoon honey
- ½ teaspoons salt
- ½ teaspoons black pepper
- ½ teaspoons crushed red pepper flakes
- 1 can (28g) chickpeas, drained
- 1 teaspoon ground cumin
- ½ teaspoons salt
- ½ teaspoons garlic powder
- ½ teaspoons ground ginger
- 1 large egg
- ½ teaspoons baking soda
- ½ cup fresh coriander, chopped
- 2 green onions, sliced

Preparation:

1. Mash chickpeas with rest of the ingredients in a food processor.
2. Layer the air fryer basket with a parchment paper.
3. Drop the batter in the basket spoon by spoon.
4. Return the air fryer basket to the Ninja Max XL Air Fryer.
5. Choose the "Max Crisp" mode at 400 degrees F and 6 minutes of cooking time.
6. Initiate cooking by pressing the START/STOP BUTTON.
7. Flip the fritters once cooked halfway through.
8. Serve warm.

Serving Suggestion: Serve with tomato ketchup and sautéed green vegetables

Variation Tip: Add sautéed onions and carrots to the batter

Nutritional Information Per Serving:
Calories 284 | Fat 7.9g |Sodium 704mg | Carbs 38.1g | Fiber 1.9g | Sugar 1.9g | Protein 14.8g

Herb and Lemon Cauliflower

Prep Time: 10 minutes.

Cook Time: 10 minutes.

Serves: 4

Ingredients:

- 1 cauliflower head, cut into florets
- 4 tablespoons olive oil
- ¼ cup fresh parsley
- 1 tablespoon fresh rosemary
- 1 tablespoon fresh thyme
- 1 teaspoon lemon zest, grated
- 2 tablespoons lemon juice
- ½ teaspoons salt
- ¼ teaspoon crushed red pepper flakes

Preparation:

1. Toss cauliflower with oil, herbs and the rest of the ingredients in a suitable bowl.

2. Add the seasoned cauliflower in the air fryer basket.

3. Return the air fryer basket to the Ninja Max XL Air Fryer.

4. Choose the "Air Fry" mode at 350 degrees F and 10 minutes of cooking time.

5. Initiate cooking by pressing the START/STOP BUTTON.

6. Serve warm.

Serving Suggestion: Serve with red chunky salsa or chili sauce

Variation Tip: Add a drop of hot sauce or a pinch of paprika for extra spice.

Nutritional Information Per Serving:

Calories 212 | Fat 11.8g |Sodium 321mg | Carbs 24.6g | Fiber 4.4g | Sugar 8g | Protein 7.3g

Mushroom Roll-Ups

Prep Time: 15 minutes.

Cook Time: 11 minutes..

Serves: 10

Ingredients:

- 2 tablespoons olive oil
- 227g portobello mushrooms, chopped

- 1 teaspoon dried oregano
- 1 teaspoon dried thyme
- ½ teaspoons crushed red pepper flakes
- ¼ teaspoon salt
- 1 package (227g) cream cheese, softened
- 113g whole-milk ricotta cheese
- 10 (8 inches) flour tortillas
- Cooking spray
- Chutney

Preparation:

1. Sauté mushrooms with oil, thyme, salt, pepper flakes, and oregano in a skillet for 4 minutes..

2. Mix cheeses and add sauteed mushrooms the mix well.

3. Add the mushroom mixture over the tortillas.

4. Roll the tortillas and secure with a toothpick.

5. Place the rolls in the air fryer basket.

6. Return the air fryer basket to the Ninja Max XL Air Fryer.

7. Choose the "Air Fry" mode and set the temperature to 400 degrees F and 11 minutes of cooking time.

8. Initiate cooking by pressing the START/STOP BUTTON.

9. Flip the rolls once cooked halfway through.

10. Serve warm.

Serving Suggestion: Serve with chili sauce

Variation Tip: Add chopped celery and carrots to the filling

Nutritional Information Per Serving:
Calories 288 | Fat 6.9g |Sodium 761mg |

Carbs 46g | Fiber 4g | Sugar 12g | Protein 9.6g

Acorn Squash Slices

Prep Time: 15 minutes.
Cook Time: 10 minutes.
Serves: 6

Ingredients:

- 2 medium acorn squashes
- ⅔ cup packed brown sugar
- ½ cup butter, melted

Preparation:

1. Cut the acorn squashes in half, remove the seeds and slice into ½ inch slices.

2. Place the squash slices in the air fryer basket.

3. Drizzle brown sugar and butter over the squash slices.

4. Return the air fryer basket to the Ninja Max XL Air Fryer.

5. Choose the "Air Fry" mode and set the temperature to 350 degrees F and 10 minutes of cooking time.

6. Initiate cooking by pressing the START/STOP BUTTON.

7. Flip the squash once cooked halfway through.

8. Serve.

Serving Suggestion: Serve with mayo sauce or ketchup

Variation Tip: Use some honey to replace brown sugar in the recipe

Nutritional Information Per Serving:

Calories 206 | Fat 3.4g |Sodium 174mg | Carbs 35g | Fiber 9.4g | Sugar 5.9g | Protein 10.6g

Bacon Wrapped Corn Cob

Prep Time: 15 minutes.
Cook Time: 10 minutes.
Serves: 4

Ingredients:

- 4 trimmed corns on the cob
- 8 bacon slices

Preparation:

1. Wrap the corn cobs with two bacon slices.
2. Place the wrapped cobs into the Ninja Air fryer basket.
3. Return the air fryer basket to the Ninja Max XL Air Fryer.
4. Choose the "Air Fry" mode and set the temperature to 355 degrees F and 10 minutes of cooking time.
5. Initiate cooking by pressing the START/STOP BUTTON.
6. Flip the corn cob once cooked halfway through.
7. Serve warm.

Serving Suggestion: Serve with mayonnaise or cream cheese dip

Variation Tip: Brush honey or maple syrup over the bacon before cooking

Nutritional Information Per Serving:

Calories 350 | Fat 2.6g |Sodium 358mg | Carbs 64.6g | Fiber 14.4g | Sugar 3.3g | Protein 19.9g

Air Fryer Vegetables

Prep Time: 15 minutes.

Cook Time: 15 minutes.

Serves: 2

Ingredients:

- 1 courgetti, diced
- 2 capsicums, diced
- 1 head broccoli, diced
- 1 red onion, diced

Marinade

- 1 teaspoon smoked paprika
- 1 teaspoon garlic granules
- 1 teaspoon Herb de Provence
- Salt and black pepper, to taste
- 1½ tablespoon olive oil
- 2 tablespoons lemon juice

Preparation:

1. Toss the broccoli and veggies with the rest of the marinade ingredients in a suitable bowl.

2. Spread the veggies in the air fryer basket.

3. Return the air fryer basket to the Ninja Max XL Air Fryer.

4. Choose the "Max Crisp" mode at 400 degrees F and 15 minutes of cooking time.

5. Initiate cooking by pressing the START/STOP BUTTON.

6. Toss the veggies once cooked half way through.

7. Serve warm.

Serving Suggestion: Serve with flatbread or white boiled rice

Variation Tip: Drizzle parmesan on top before serving

Nutritional Information Per Serving:

Calories 166 | Fat 3.2g |Sodium 437mg | Carbs 28.8g | Fiber 1.8g | Sugar 2.7g | Protein 5.8g

Green Tomato Stacks

Prep Time: 15 minutes.

Cook Time: 12 minutes.

Serves: 6

Ingredients:

- ¼ cup mayonnaise
- ¼ teaspoon lime zest, grated
- 2 tablespoons lime juice
- 1 teaspoon minced fresh thyme
- ½ teaspoons black pepper
- ¼ cup all-purpose flour
- 2 large egg whites, beaten
- ¾ cup cornmeal
- ¼ teaspoon salt
- 2 medium green tomatoes
- 2 medium red tomatoes
- Cooking spray
- 8 slices Canadian bacon, warmed

Preparation:

1. Mix mayonnaise with ¼ teaspoon black pepper, thyme, lime juice and zest in a suitable bowl.
2. Spread flour in one bowl, beat egg whites in another bowl and mix cornmeal with ¼ teaspoon black pepper and salt in a third bowl.
3. Cut the tomatoes into 4 slices and coat each with the flour then dip in the egg whites.
4. Coat the tomatoes slices with the cornmeal mixture.
5. Place the slices in the air fryer basket.
6. Return the air fryer basket to the Ninja Max XL Air Fryer.
7. Choose the "Air Fry" mode at 390 degrees F and 12 minutes of cooking time.
8. Initiate cooking by pressing the START/STOP BUTTON.
9. Flip the tomatoes once cooked halfway through.
10. Place the green tomato slices on the working surface.
11. Top them with bacon, and red tomato slice.
12. Serve.

Serving Suggestion: Serve with yogurt dip and sautéed carrots

Variation Tip: Use breadcrumbs for breading to have extra crispiness

Nutritional Information Per Serving:

Calories 113 | Fat 3g |Sodium 152mg | Carbs 20g | Fiber 3g | Sugar 1.1g | Protein 3.5g

Air-Fried Radishes

Prep Time: 10 minutes.

Cook Time: 15 minutes.

Serves: 6

Ingredients:

- 2¼ pounds radishes, quartered
- 3 tablespoons olive oil
- 1 tablespoon fresh oregano, minced
- ¼ teaspoon salt
- ⅛ teaspoon black pepper

Preparation:

1. Toss radishes with oil, black pepper, salt and oregano in a suitable bowl.

2. Add the radishes into the Ninja Air fryer basket.

3. Return the air fryer basket to the Ninja Max XL Air Fryer.

4. Choose the "Max Crisp" mode at 375 degrees F and 15 minutes of cooking time.

5. Initiate cooking by pressing the START/STOP BUTTON.

6. Toss the radishes once cooked halfway through.

7. Serve.

Serving Suggestion: Serve with mayonnaise or cream cheese dip

Variation Tip: Add a drizzle of dried herbs before cooking

Nutritional Information Per Serving:

Calories 270 | Fat 14.6g |Sodium 394mg | Carbs 31.3g | Fiber 7.5g | Sugar 9.7g | Protein 6.4g

Garlic-Rosemary Brussels Sprouts

Prep Time: 15 minutes.

Cook Time: 8 minutes.

Serves: 4

Ingredients:

- 3 tablespoons olive oil
- 2 garlic cloves, minced
- ½ teaspoons salt
- ¼ teaspoon black pepper
- 1 pound Brussels sprouts, halved
- ½ cup panko bread crumbs
- 1-½ teaspoons rosemary, minced

Preparation:

1. Toss the Brussels sprouts with crumbs and the rest of the ingredients in a suitable bowl.

2. Add the sprouts into the Ninja Air fryer basket.

3. Return the air fryer basket to the Ninja Max XL Air Fryer.

4. Choose the "Air Fry" mode at 350 degrees F and 8 minutes of cooking time.

5. Initiate cooking by pressing the START/STOP BUTTON.

6. Toss the Brussels sprouts once cooked halfway through.

7. Serve warm.

Serving Suggestion: Serve with yogurt dip

Variation Tip: Drizzle shredded parmesan on top

Nutritional Information Per Serving:

Calories 231 | Fat 9g |Sodium 271mg | Carbs 32.8g | Fiber 6.4g | Sugar 7g | Protein 6.3g

Fried Patty Pan Squash

Prep Time: 10 minutes.

Cook Time: 15 minutes.

Serves: 6

Ingredients:

- 5 cups small pattypan squash, halved
- 1 tablespoon olive oil
- 2 garlic cloves, minced
- ½ teaspoons salt
- ¼ teaspoon dried oregano
- ¼ teaspoon dried thyme
- ¼ teaspoon pepper
- 1 tablespoon minced parsley

Preparation:

1. Rub the squash with oil, garlic and the rest of the ingredients.

2. Spread the squash in the air fryer basket.

3. Return the air fryer basket to the Ninja Max XL Air Fryer.

4. Choose the "Air Fry" mode at 375 degrees F and 15 minutes of cooking time.

5. Initiate cooking by pressing the START/STOP BUTTON.

6. Flip the squash once cooked halfway through.

7. Garnish with parsley.

8. Serve warm.

Serving Suggestion: Serve with bread slices

Variation Tip: Sprinkle cornmeal before cooking for added crisp

Nutritional Information Per Serving:

Calories 208 | Fat 5g |Sodium 1205mg | Carbs 34.1g | Fiber 7.8g | Sugar 2.5g | Protein 5.9g

Breaded Summer Squash

Prep Time: 15 minutes.

Cook Time: 10 minutes.

Serves: 4

Ingredients:

- 4 cups yellow summer squash, sliced
- 3 tablespoons olive oil
- ½ teaspoons salt
- ½ teaspoons pepper
- ⅛ teaspoon cayenne pepper
- ¾ cup panko bread crumbs
- ¾ cup grated Parmesan cheese

Preparation:

1. Mix crumbs, cheese, cayenne pepper, black pepper, salt and oil in a suitable bowl.
2. Coat the squash slices with the breadcrumb mixture.
3. Place these slices in the air fryer basket.
4. Return the air fryer basket to the Ninja Max XL Air Fryer.
5. Choose the "Air Fry" mode at 350 degrees F and 10 minutes of cooking time.
6. Initiate cooking by pressing the START/STOP BUTTON.
7. Flip the squash slices once cooked half way through.
8. Serve warm.

Serving Suggestion: Serve with red chunky salsa or chili sauce

Variation Tip: Use crushed cornflakes for breading to have extra crispiness

Nutritional Information Per Serving:
Calories 193 | Fat 1g |Sodium 395mg | Carbs 38.7g | Fiber 1.6g | Sugar 0.9g | Protein 6.6g

Crispy Parmesan Cod

Prep Time: 15 minutes.

Cook Time: 10 minutes.

Serves: 2

Ingredients:

- 453.5g cod filets
- Salt and black pepper, to taste
- ½ cup flour
- 2 large eggs, beaten
- ½ teaspoons salt
- 1 cup Panko
- ½ cup grated parmesan
- 2 teaspoons old bay seasoning
- ½ teaspoons garlic powder
- Olive oil spray

Preparation:

1. Rub the cod fillets with black pepper and salt.
2. Mix panko with parmesan cheese, old bay seasoning, and garlic powder in a suitable bowl.
3. Mix flour with salt in another bowl.
4. Dredge the cod filets in the flour then dip in the eggs and coat with the Panko mixture.
5. Place the cod fillets in the air fryer basket.
6. Return the air fryer basket to the Ninja Max XL Air Fryer.
7. Choose the "Air Fry" mode and set the temperature to 400 degrees F and 10 minutes of cooking time.
8. Initiate cooking by pressing the START/STOP BUTTON.
9. Flip the cod fillets once cooked halfway through.
10. Serve warm.

Serving Suggestion: Serve with sauteed asparagus sticks

Variation Tip: Use crushed cornflakes for breading to have extra crispiness

Nutritional Information Per Serving:

Calories 275 | Fat 1.4g |Sodium 582mg | Carbs 31.5g | Fiber 1.1g | Sugar 0.1g | Protein 29.8g

Tuna Steaks

Prep Time: 15 minutes.

Cook Time: 30 minutes.

Serves: 2

Ingredients:

- 2 (6 ounce) boneless tuna steaks
- ¼ cup soy sauce
- 2 teaspoons honey
- 1 teaspoon grated ginger
- 1 teaspoon sesame oil
- ½ teaspoons rice vinegar

Preparation:

1. Mix rice vinegar, sesame oil, ginger, honey and soy sauce in a suitable bowl.

2. Pour this marinade over the tuna steaks and cover to marinate for 30 minutes..

3. Place the tuna steaks in the air fryer basket in a single layer.

4. Return the air fryer basket to the Ninja Max XL Air Fryer.

5. Choose the "Air Fry" mode and set the temperature to 380 degrees F and 4 minutes of cooking time.

6. Initiate cooking by pressing the START/STOP BUTTON.

7. Serve warm.

Serving Suggestion: Serve with sautéed or fresh greens with melted butter

Variation Tip: Drizzle lemon juice on top before serving

Nutritional Information Per Serving:

Calories 348 | Fat 30g |Sodium 660mg | Carbs 5g | Fiber 0g | Sugar 0g | Protein 14g

Shrimp with Lemon and Pepper

Prep Time: 10 minutes.

Cook Time: 8 minutes.

Serves: 4

Ingredients:

- 453.5g raw shrimp, peeled and deveined
- 118ml olive oil
- 2 tablespoons lemon juice
- 1 teaspoon black pepper
- ½ teaspoons salt

Preparation:

1. Toss shrimp with black pepper, salt, lemon juice and oil in a suitable bowl.
2. Add the shrimp into the Ninja Air fryer basket.
3. Return the air fryer basket to the Ninja Max XL Air Fryer.
4. Choose the "Air Fry" mode at 350 degrees F and 8 minutes of cooking time.
5. Initiate cooking by pressing the START/STOP BUTTON.
6. Serve warm.

Serving Suggestion: Serve on a bed of boiled pasta

Variation Tip: Drizzle shredded parmesan on top before serving

Nutritional Information Per Serving:

Calories 257 | Fat 10.4g |Sodium 431mg | Carbs 20g | Fiber 0g | Sugar 1.6g | Protein 21g

Furikake Salmon

Prep Time: 20 minutes.

Cook Time: 10 minutes.

Serves: 4

Ingredients:

- ½ cup mayonnaise
- 1 tablespoon shoyu
- 1 pound salmon fillet
- Salt and black pepper to taste
- 2 tablespoons furikake

Preparation:

1. Mix shoyu with mayonnaise in a small bowl.
2. Rub the salmon with black pepper and salt.
3. Place the salmon pieces in the air fryer basket.
4. Top them with the mayo mixture.
5. Return the air fryer basket to the Ninja Max XL Air Fryer.
6. Choose the "Air Fry" mode at 400 degrees F and 10 minutes of cooking time.

7. Initiate cooking by pressing the START/STOP BUTTON.

8. Serve warm.

Serving Suggestion: Serve on top of mashed potato or mashed cauliflower

Variation Tip: Use crushed cornflakes for breading to have extra crispiness

Nutritional Information Per Serving:
Calories 297 | Fat 1g |Sodium 291mg | Carbs 35g | Fiber 1g | Sugar 9g | Protein 29g

Cajun Scallops

Prep Time: 15 minutes.

Cook Time: 6 minutes.

Serves: 6

Ingredients:

- 6 sea scallops
- Cooking spray
- Salt to taste
- Cajun seasoning

Preparation:

1. Season the scallops with Cajun seasoning and salt.

2. Place them in one air fryer basket and spray them with cooking oil.

3. Return the air fryer basket of the Ninja Max XL Air Fryer.

4. Choose the "Air Fry" mode and set the temperature to 400 degrees F and 6 minutes of cooking time.

5. Initiate cooking by pressing the START/STOP BUTTON.

6. Flip the scallops once cooked halfway through.

7. Serve warm.

Serving Suggestion: Serve with fresh cucumber salad

Variation Tip: Use crushed cornflakes for breading to have extra crispiness

Nutritional Information Per Serving:
Calories 266 | Fat 6.3g |Sodium 193mg | Carbs 39.1g | Fiber 7.2g | Sugar 5.2g | Protein 14.8g

Stuffed Mushrooms with Crab

Prep Time: 15 minutes.

Cook Time: 18 minutes.

Serves: 4

Ingredients:

- 907g baby bella mushrooms
- cooking spray
- 2 teaspoons tony chachere's salt blend
- ¼ red onion, diced
- 2 celery ribs, diced
- 227g lump crab
- ½ cup seasoned bread crumbs
- 1 large egg
- ½ cup parmesan cheese, shredded
- 1 teaspoon oregano
- 1 teaspoon hot sauce

Preparation:

1. Mix all the ingredients except the mushrooms in a suitable bowl.
2. Add the crab filling into the mushroom caps.
3. Place the caps in the air fryer basket.
4. Return the air fryer basket to the Ninja Max XL Air Fryer.
5. Choose the "Air Fry" mode at 400 degrees F and 18 minutes of cooking time.
6. Initiate cooking by pressing the START/STOP BUTTON.
7. Serve warm.

Serving Suggestion: Serve with pasta or fried rice

Variation Tip: Drizzle parmesan cheese on top

Nutritional Information Per Serving:

Calories 399 | Fat 16g |Sodium 537mg | Carbs 28g | Fiber 3g | Sugar 10g | Protein 35

Brown Sugar Garlic Salmon

Prep Time: 15 minutes.

Cook Time: 10 minutes.

Serves: 4

Ingredients:

- 1 pound salmon
- Salt and black pepper, to taste
- 2 tablespoons brown sugar
- 1 teaspoon chili powder
- ½ teaspoons paprika
- 1 teaspoon Italian seasoning
- 1 teaspoon garlic powder

Preparation:

1. Mix brown sugar with garlic powder, Italian seasoning, paprika, and chili powder in a suitable bowl.

2. Rub this mixture over the salmon along with black pepper and salt.

3. Place the salmon in the air fryer basket.

4. Return the air fryer basket to the Ninja Max XL Air Fryer.

5. Choose the "Air Fry" mode and set the temperature to 400 degrees F and 10 minutes of cooking time.

6. Initiate cooking by pressing the START/STOP BUTTON.

7. Flip the salmon once cooked halfway through.

8. Serve warm.

Serving Suggestion: Serve with sauteed asparagus sticks

Variation Tip: Rub with a teaspoon of lemon juice before seasoning

Nutritional Information Per Serving:

Calories 275 | Fat 1.4g |Sodium 582mg | Carbs 31.5g | Fiber 1.1g | Sugar 0.1g | Protein 29.8g

Honey Teriyaki Salmon

Prep Time: 15 minutes.

Cook Time: 12 minutes.

Serves: 3

Ingredients:

- 8 tablespoon teriyaki sauce
- 3 tablespoons honey
- 2 cubes frozen garlic
- 2 tablespoons olive oil
- 3 pieces wild salmon

Preparation:

1. Mix teriyaki sauce, honey, garlic and oil in a large bowl.

2. Add salmon to this sauce and mix well to coat.

3. Cover and refrigerate the salmon for 20 minutes..

4. Place the salmon pieces in one air fryer basket.

5. Return the air fryer basket of the Ninja Max XL Air Fryer.

6. Choose the "Max Crisp" mode and set the temperature to 350 degrees F and 12 minutes of cooking time.

7. Initiate cooking by pressing the START/STOP BUTTON.

8. Flip the pieces once cooked halfway through.

9. Serve warm.

Serving Suggestion: Serve with sautéed green beans or asparagus

Variation Tip: Add lemon juice to the fish before seasoning

Nutritional Information Per Serving:

Calories 260 | Fat 16g |Sodium 585mg |

Carbs 3.1g | Fiber 1.3g | Sugar 0.2g | Protein 25.5g

Foil Packet Salmon

Prep Time: 10 minutes.

Cook Time: 14 minutes.

Serves: 4

Ingredients:

- 453.5g salmon fillets
- 4 cups green beans defrosted
- 4 tablespoons soy sauce
- 2 tablespoons honey
- 2 teaspoons sesame seeds
- 1 teaspoon garlic powder
- ½ teaspoon ginger powder
- ½ teaspoon salt
- ¼ teaspoon white pepper
- ¼ teaspoon red pepper flakes
- Salt, to taste
- Canola oil spray

Preparation:

1. Make 4 foil packets and adjust the salmon fillets in each.
2. Add the green beans in the foil packets and drizzle half of the spices on top.
3. Place one salmon piece on top of each and drizzle the remaining ingredients on top.
4. Pack the salmon with the foil and place the packets in the air fryer basket.
5. Return the air fryer basket to the Ninja Max XL Air Fryer.
6. Choose the "Max Crisp" mode and set the temperature to 425 degrees F and 14 minutes of cooking time.
7. Initiate cooking by pressing the START/STOP BUTTON.
8. Serve warm.

Serving Suggestion: Serve with melted butter on top

Variation Tip: Rub the salmon with lemon juice before cooking.

Nutritional Information Per Serving:
Calories 305 | Fat 15g |Sodium 482mg | Carbs 17g | Fiber 3g | Sugar 2g | Protein 35g

Pretzel-Crusted Catfish

Prep Time: 20 minutes.

Cook Time: 12 minutes.

Serves: 4

Ingredients:

- 4 catfish fillets
- ½ teaspoons salt
- ½ teaspoons black pepper
- 2 large eggs
- ⅓ cup Dijon mustard
- 2 tablespoons 2 percent milk
- ½ cup all-purpose flour
- 4 cups miniature pretzels, crushed
- Cooking spray
- Lemon slices

Preparation:

1. Rub the catfish with black pepper and salt.
2. Beat eggs with milk and mustard in a suitable bowl.
3. Spread pretzels and flour in two separate bowls.
4. Coat the catfish with flour then dip in the egg mixture and coat with the pretzels.
5. Place those spiced fish fillets in the air fryer basket.
6. Return the air fryer basket to the Ninja Max XL Air Fryer.
7. Choose the "Air Fry" mode at 325 degrees F and 12 minutes of cooking time.
8. Initiate cooking by pressing the START/STOP BUTTON.
9. Serve warm.

Serving Suggestion: Serve with sautéed cauliflower on the side

Variation Tip: Dip the fish in buttermilk before breading and air frying

Nutritional Information Per Serving:

Calories 196 | Fat 7.1g |Sodium 492mg | Carbs 21.6g | Fiber 2.9g | Sugar 0.8g | Protein 13.4g

Chili Lime Tilapia

Prep Time: 15 minutes.

Cook Time: 10 minutes.

Serves: 4

Ingredients:

- 340g tilapia fillets
- 2 teaspoons chili powder
- 1 teaspoon cumin
- 1 teaspoon garlic powder
- ½ teaspoons oregano
- ½ teaspoons sea salt
- ¼ teaspoon black pepper
- Lime zest from 1 lime
- Juice of ½ lime

Preparation:

1. Mix chili powder and other spices with lime juice and zest in a suitable bowl.
2. Rub this spice mixture over the tilapia fillets.
3. Place the spiced fillets in the air basket.
4. Return the air fryer basket to the Ninja Max XL Air Fryer.
5. Choose the "Air Fry" mode at 400 degrees F and 10 minutes of cooking time.
6. Initiate cooking by pressing the START/STOP BUTTON.
7. Flip the tilapia fillets once cooked halfway through.
8. Serve warm.

Serving Suggestion: Serve with sauteed broccoli florets

Variation Tip: Use crushed cornflakes for breading to have extra crispiness

Nutritional Information Per Serving:
Calories 275 | Fat 1.4g |Sodium 582mg | Carbs 31.5g | Fiber 1.1g | Sugar 0.1g | Protein 29.8g

Air Fryer Calamari

Prep Time: 10 minutes.
Cook Time: 7 minutes.
Serves: 4

Ingredients:

- ½ cup all-purpose flour
- 1 large egg
- 59ml milk
- 2 cups panko bread crumbs
- 1 teaspoon sea salt
- 1 teaspoon black pepper
- 1-pound calamari rings
- nonstick cooking spray

Preparation:

1. Beat egg with milk in a suitable bowl.
2. Mix flour with black pepper and salt in a suitable bowl.
3. Coat the calamari rings with the flour mixture then dip in the egg mixture and coat with the breadcrumbs.
4. Place the coated calamari in the air fryer basket.
5. Return the air fryer basket to the Ninja Max XL Air Fryer.
6. Choose the "Air Fry" mode at 400 degrees F and 7 minutes of cooking time.
7. Initiate cooking by pressing the START/STOP BUTTON.
8. Flip the calamari rings once cooked half way through.
9. Serve warm.

Serving Suggestion: Serve with parsley and melted butter on top

Variation Tip: Rub the calamari rings with lemon juice before cooking

Nutritional Information Per Serving:

Calories 336 | Fat 6g |Sodium 181mg | Carbs 1.3g | Fiber 0.2g | Sugar 0.4g | Protein 69.2g

Honey Pecan Shrimp

Prep Time: 15 minutes.

Cook Time: 10 minutes.

Serves: 4

Ingredients:

- ¼ cup cornstarch
- ¾ teaspoon salt
- ¼ teaspoon black pepper
- 2 egg whites
- ⅔ cup pecans, chopped
- 453.5g shrimp, peeled, and deveined
- ¼ cup honey
- 2 tablespoons mayonnaise

Preparation:

1. Mix cornstarch with ½ teaspoon black pepper, and ½ teaspoon salt in a suitable bowl.
2. Mix pecans and ¼ teaspoon salt in another bowl.
3. Beat egg whites in another bowl.
4. Dredge the shrimp through the cornstarch mixture then dip in the egg whites.
5. Coat the shrimp with pecans mixture.
6. Add the coated shrimp in the air fryer basket.
7. Return the air fryer basket to the Ninja Max XL Air Fryer.
8. Choose the "Air Fry" mode at 330 degrees F and 10 minutes of cooking time.
9. Initiate cooking by pressing the START/STOP BUTTON.
10. Flip the shrimps once cooked halfway through.
11. Serve.

Serving Suggestion: Enjoy with creamy coleslaw on the side

Variation Tip: Use almonds or walnuts instead of pecans

Nutritional Information Per Serving:

Calories 155 | Fat 4.2g |Sodium 963mg | Carbs 21.5g | Fiber 0.8g | Sugar 5.7g | Protein 8.1g

Crumb-Topped Sole

Prep Time: 15 minutes.

Cook Time: 7 minutes.

Serves: 4

Ingredients:

- 3 tablespoons mayonnaise
- 3 tablespoons Parmesan cheese, grated
- 2 teaspoons mustard seeds
- ¼ teaspoon black pepper
- 4 (170g) sole fillets
- 1 cup soft bread crumbs
- 1 green onion, chopped
- ½ teaspoons ground mustard
- 2 teaspoons butter, melted
- Cooking spray

Preparation:

1. Mix mayonnaise with black pepper, mustard seeds, and 2 tablespoons cheese in a suitable bowl.

2. Place 2 sole fillets in the air fryer basket and top them with mayo mixture.

3. Mix breadcrumbs with rest of the ingredients in a suitable bowl.

4. Drizzle this mixture over the sole fillets.

5. Return the air fryer basket to the Ninja Max XL Air Fryer.

6. Choose the "Air Fry" mode and set the temperature to 375 degrees F and 7 minutes of cooking time.

7. Initiate cooking by pressing the START/STOP BUTTON.

8. Serve warm.

Serving Suggestion: Serve with melted butter on top

Variation Tip: Drizzle shredded parmesan on top before air frying

Nutritional Information Per Serving:

Calories 308 | Fat 24g |Sodium 715mg | Carbs 0.8g | Fiber 0.1g | Sugar 0.1g | Protein 21.9g

Bacon Wrapped Stuffed Chicken

Prep Time: 15 minutes.

Cook Time: 25 minutes.

Serves: 4

Ingredients:

- 3 boneless chicken breasts
- 6 jalapenos, sliced
- ¾ cup (170g) cream cheese
- ½ cup Monterey Jack cheese, shredded
- 1 teaspoon ground cumin
- 12 strips thick bacon

Preparation:

1. Cut the cleaned chicken breasts in half crosswise and pound them with a mallet.
2. Mix cream cheese with cumin and Monterey jacket cheese in a suitable bowl.
3. Spread the cream cheese mixture over the chicken breast slices.
4. Add jalapeno slices on top and wrap the chicken slices.
5. Wrap each chicken rolls with a bacon slice.
6. Place the wrapped rolls into the Ninja Air fryer basket.
7. Return the air fryer basket to the Ninja Max XL Air Fryer.
8. Choose the "Air Fry" mode at 340 degrees F and 25 minutes of cooking time.
9. Initiate cooking by pressing the START/STOP BUTTON.
10. Serve warm.

Serving Suggestion: Serve with fried rice and green beans salad

Variation Tip: Coat the chicken with crushed cornflakes for extra crispiness

Nutritional Information Per Serving:

Calories 220 | Fat 1.7g | Sodium 178mg | Carbs 1.7g | Fiber 0.2g | Sugar 0.2g | Protein 32.9g

Crispy Sesame Chicken

Prep Time: 20 minutes.

Cook Time: 10 minutes.

Serves: 2

Ingredients:

- 1½ pounds boneless chicken thighs, diced
- 2 tablespoons rice vinegar
- 1 tablespoon soy sauce
- 2 teaspoons minced fresh ginger
- 1 garlic clove, minced
- ¾ teaspoon salt
- ½ teaspoon black pepper
- 2 large eggs, beaten
- 1 cup cornstarch

Sauce

- 59ml soy sauce
- 2 tablespoons rice vinegar
- ⅓ cup brown sugar
- 59ml water
- 1 tablespoon cornstarch
- 2 teaspoons sesame oil
- 2 tablespoons vegetable oil
- 2 garlic cloves, minced
- 2 teaspoons chile paste

Garnish

- 1 tablespoon toasted sesame seeds

Preparation:

1. Blend all the sauce ingredients in a saucepan and cook until it thickens then allow it to cool.

2. Mix chicken with black pepper, salt, garlic, ginger, vinegar, and soy sauce in a suitable bowl.

3. Cover and marinate the chicken for 20 minutes..

4. Add the chicken in the air fryer basket.

5. Return the air fryer basket to the Ninja Max XL Air Fryer.

6. Choose the "Air Fry" mode and set the temperature to 400 degrees F and 10 minutes of cooking time.

7. Initiate cooking by pressing the START/STOP BUTTON.

8. Pour the prepared sauce over the air fried chicken and drizzle sesame seeds on top.

9. Serve warm.

Serving Suggestion: Serve with boiled white rice or chow mein

Variation Tip: You can use honey instead of sugar to sweeten the sauce

Nutritional Information Per Serving:
Calories 351 | Fat 16g |Sodium 777mg | Carbs 26g | Fiber 4g | Sugar 5g | Protein 28g

Pretzel Chicken Cordon Bleu

Prep Time: 10 minutes.

Cook Time: 26 minutes.

Serves: 4

Ingredients:

- 5 boneless chicken thighs
- 3 cups pretzels, crushed
- 2 eggs, beaten
- 10 deli honey ham, slices
- 5 Swiss cheese slices
- Cooking spray

Preparation:

1. Grind pretzels in a food processor.
2. Pound the chicken tights with a mallet.
3. Top each chicken piece with one cheese slice and 2 ham slices.
4. Roll the chicken pieces and secure with a toothpick.
5. Dip the rolls in the eggs and coat with the breadcrumbs.
6. Place these rolls in the air fryer basket.
7. Spray them with cooking oil.
8. Return the air fryer basket to the Ninja Max XL Air Fryer.
9. Choose the "Air Fry" mode and set the temperature to 375 degrees F and 26 minutes of cooking time.
10. Initiate cooking by pressing the START/STOP BUTTON.
11. Flip the rolls once cooked halfway through.
12. Serve warm.

Serving Suggestion: Serve with fresh rocket leaves salad

Variation Tip: Drizzle mixed dried herbs on top before cooking

Nutritional Information Per Serving:
Calories 380 | Fat 29g |Sodium 821mg | Carbs 34.6g | Fiber 0g | Sugar 0g | Protein 30g

Jamaican Fried Chicken

Prep Time: 15 minutes.
Cook Time: 25 minutes.
Serves: 6

Ingredients:

- 6-8 chicken thighs

Egg Marinade:

- 2 teaspoons of hot sauce
- 1 teaspoon of ground ginger
- 1 teaspoon of ground onion
- 1 teaspoon of black pepper
- 1 teaspoon of ground garlic
- 237ml of almond milk
- 1 tablespoon of lemon juice
- 1 large egg

Breading:

- 2 cups of ground almonds
- ⅓ cup of tapioca starch

- 1 tablespoon of paprika
- 1 tablespoon of thyme
- 1 tablespoon of parsley
- 1 teaspoon of garlic powder
- 1 teaspoon of onion powder
- ½ teaspoon of cayenne pepper
- 1 teaspoon of pink salt
- Spray on cooking oil olive oil spray

Preparation:

1. Mix egg marinade ingredients in a large bowl and add chicken thighs.
2. Stir well to coat then cover and refrigerate for 30 minutes..
3. Meanwhile, mix all the breading ingredients in a shallow bowl.
4. Remove the chicken from the egg marinade and coat with the breading mixture.
5. Place the coated chicken thighs in the air fryer basket.
6. Return the air fryer basket to the Ninja Max XL Air Fryer.
7. Choose the "Max Crisp" mode and set the temperature to 375 degrees F and 25 minutes of cooking time.
8. Initiate cooking by pressing the START/STOP BUTTON.
9. Flip the chicken thighs once cooked halfway through.
10. Serve.

Serving Suggestion: Serve with cucumber salad and warm bread

Variation Tip: Rub the chicken with lemon juice before seasoning

Nutritional Information Per Serving:
Calories 268 | Fat 10.4g |Sodium 411mg | Carbs 0.4g | Fiber 0.1g | Sugar 0.1g | Protein 40.6g

Chicken Kebabs

Prep Time: 15 minutes.
Cook Time: 9 minutes.
Serves: 4

Ingredients:

- 453.5g boneless chicken breast, cut into 1-inch pieces
- 1 tablespoon avocado oil
- 1 tablespoon Tamari soy sauce
- 1 teaspoon garlic powder
- 1 teaspoon ground ginger
- 1 teaspoon chili powder
- 1 tablespoon honey
- 1 green capsicum, cut into 1-inch pieces
- 1 red capsicum, cut into 1-inch pieces
- 1 yellow capsicum, cut into 1-inch pieces

- 1 courgetti, cut into 1-inch pieces
- 1 red onion, cut into 1-inch pieces
- cooking spray

Preparation:

1. Rub cleaned chicken with oil and place in a suitable bowl.
2. Mix honey, chili powder, ginger, garlic and soy sauce in a suitable bowl.
3. Pour this mixture over the chicken.
4. Cover and marinate the chicken for 15 minutes..
5. Thread the marinated chicken with veggies on wooden skewers alternately.
6. Add the skewers and place in the air fryer basket.
7. Return the air fryer basket to the Ninja Max XL Air Fryer.
8. Choose the "Air Fry" mode at 350 degrees F and 9 minutes of cooking time.
9. Initiate cooking by pressing the START/STOP BUTTON.
10. Flip the skewers once cooked halfway through.
11. Serve warm.

Serving Suggestion: Serve with white rice and avocado salad

Variation Tip: Rub the chicken breast with lemon juice before seasoning

Nutritional Information Per Serving:
Calories 546 | Fat 33.1g |Sodium 1201mg | Carbs 30g | Fiber 2.4g | Sugar 9.7g | Protein 32g

Cornish Hen

Prep Time: 20 minutes.
Cook Time: 35 minutes.
Serves: 4

Ingredients:

- 2 Cornish hens
- 2 tablespoons olive oil
- 2 teaspoons salt
- 1½ teaspoons Italian seasoning
- 1 teaspoon garlic powder
- 1 teaspoon paprika
- ½ teaspoons black pepper
- ½ teaspoons lemon zest

Preparation:

1. Mix Italian seasoning with lemon zest, juice, black pepper, paprika, and garlic powder in a suitable bowl.

2. Rub each hen with the seasoning mixture.

3. Tuck the hen wings in and place one in the air fryer basket.

4. Return the air fryer basket to the Ninja Max XL Air Fryer.

5. Choose the "Air Fry" mode and set the temperature to 375 degrees F and 35 minutes of cooking time.

6. Initiate cooking by pressing the START/STOP BUTTON.

7. Flip the hens once cooked halfway through.

8. Serve warm.

Serving Suggestion: Serve with warm corn tortilla and cucumber salad

Variation Tip: Rub the hens with lemon or orange juice before seasoning

Nutritional Information Per Serving:

Calories 223 | Fat 11.7g |Sodium 721mg | Carbs 13.6g | Fiber 0.7g | Sugar 8g | Protein 15.7g

Crispy Fried Quail

Prep Time: 15 minutes.

Cook Time: 6 minutes.

Serves: 8

Ingredients:

- 8 boneless quail breasts
- 2 tablespoons Sichuan pepper dry rub mix
- ¾ cup rice flour
- ¼ cup all-purpose flour
- 2-3 cups peanut oil

Garnish

- Sliced jalapenos
- Fresh lime wedges
- Fresh coriander

Preparation:

1. Split the quail breasts in half.

2. Mix Sichuan mix with flours in a suitable bowl.

3. Coat the quail breasts with flour mixture and place in the air fryer basket.

4. Return the air fryer basket to the Ninja Max XL Air Fryer.

5. Choose the "Max Crisp" mode at 300 degrees F and 6 minutes of cooking time.

6. Initiate cooking by pressing the START/STOP BUTTON.

7. Flip the quail breasts once cooked halfway through.

8. Serve warm.

Serving Suggestion: Serve quail breasts with chopped jalapenos on top

Variation Tip: Coat the quail with seasoned parmesan before cooking

Nutritional Information Per Serving:

Calories 351 | Fat 11g |Sodium 150mg |

Carbs 3.3g | Fiber 0.2g | Sugar 1g | Protein 33.2g

Chicken and Potatoes

Prep Time: 15 minutes.

Cook Time: 10 minutes.

Serves: 2

Ingredients:

- 2 potatoes, diced
- 2 chicken breasts, diced
- 4 cloves garlic crushed
- 2 teaspoons smoked paprika
- ½ teaspoon red chili flakes
- 1 teaspoon fresh thyme
- 1 teaspoon salt
- ¼ teaspoon black pepper
- 2 tablespoons olive oil

Preparation:

1. Rub chicken with half of the salt, black pepper, oil, thyme, red chili flakes, paprika and garlic.
2. Mix potatoes with remaining spices, oil and garlic in a suitable bowl.
3. Add chicken to one air fryer basket and potatoes the second basket.
4. Return the air fryer basket to the Ninja Max XL Air Fryer.
5. Choose the "Air Fry" mode at 375 degrees F and 10 minutes of cooking time.
6. Initiate cooking by pressing the START/STOP BUTTON.
7. Flip the chicken and toss potatoes once cooked halfway through.
8. Garnish with chopped parsley.
9. Serve chicken with the potatoes.

Serving Suggestion: Serve with tomato soup on the side

Variation Tip: Use shredded parmesan to coat the chicken to have extra crispiness

Nutritional Information Per Serving:

Calories 374 | Fat 13g |Sodium 552mg | Carbs 25g | Fiber 1.2g | Sugar 1.2g | Protein 37.7g

Air Fried Chicken Legs

Prep Time: 15 minutes.

Cook Time: 10 minutes.

Serves: 4

Ingredients:

- 8 chicken legs
- 2 tablespoons olive oil
- 1 teaspoon salt
- 1 teaspoon black pepper
- 1 teaspoon smoked paprika
- 1 teaspoon garlic powder
- 1 teaspoon dried parsley

Preparation:

1. Mix chicken with oil, herbs and spices in a suitable bowl.

2. Add the chicken legs in the air fryer basket.

3. Return the air fryer basket to the Ninja Max XL Air Fryer.

4. Choose the "Air Fry" mode at 400 degrees F and 10 minutes of cooking time.

5. Initiate cooking by pressing the START/STOP BUTTON.

6. Flip the chicken once cooked halfway through.

7. Serve warm.

Serving Suggestion: Serve with fresh-cut tomatoes and sautéed greens

Variation Tip: Rub the chicken with lemon juice before seasoning

Nutritional Information Per Serving:

Calories 220 | Fat 13g |Sodium 542mg | Carbs 0.9g | Fiber 0.3g | Sugar 0.2g | Protein 25.6g

Thai Curry Chicken Kabobs

Prep Time: 15 minutes.

Cook Time: 15 minutes.

Serves: 4

Ingredients:

- 900g skinless chicken thighs

- 120ml Tamari
- 60ml coconut milk
- 3 tablespoons lime juice
- 3 tablespoons maple syrup
- 2 tablespoons Thai red curry

Preparation:

1. Mix red curry paste, honey, lime juice, coconut milk, soy sauce in a suitable bowl.
2. Add this sauce and chicken to a Ziplock bag.
3. Seal the bag and shake it to coat well.
4. Refrigerate the chicken for 2 hours then thread the chicken over wooden skewers.
5. Add the skewers in the air fryer basket.
6. Return the air fryer basket to the Ninja Max XL Air Fryer.
7. Choose the "Air Fry" mode at 350 F and 15 minutes of cooking time.
8. Initiate cooking by pressing the START/STOP BUTTON.
9. Flip the skewers once cooked halfway through.
10. Serve warm.

Serving Suggestion: Serve with warm corn tortilla and Greek salad

Variation Tip: You can use the almond milk as well

Nutritional Information Per Serving:

Calories 353 | Fat 5g |Sodium 818mg | Carbs 53.2g | Fiber 4.4g | Sugar 8g | Protein 17.3g

Chicken Caprese

Prep Time: 10 minutes.

Cook Time: 10 minutes.

Serves: 4

Ingredients:

- 4 chicken breast cutlets
- 1 teaspoon Italian seasoning
- 1 teaspoon salt
- ½ teaspoons black pepper
- 4 slices fresh mozzarella cheese
- 1 large tomato, sliced
- Basil and balsamic vinegar to garnish

Preparation:

1. Pat dry the chicken cutlets with a kitchen towel.
2. Rub the chicken with Italian seasoning, black pepper and salt.
3. Place those spiced chicken breasts in the air fryer basket.
4. Return the air fryer basket to the Ninja Max XL Air Fryer.

5. Choose the "Air Fry" mode at 375 degrees F and 10 minutes of cooking time.

6. Initiate cooking by pressing the START/STOP BUTTON.

7. After 10 minutes, top each cooked chicken breast with a slice of cheese and tomato slices.

8. Return the basket to the Ninja Max XL Air Fryer and air fry for 5 another minutes..

9. Garnish with balsamic vinegar and basil.

10. Serve warm.

Serving Suggestion: Serve with warm corn tortilla and Greek salad

Variation Tip: Coat and dust the chicken breast with flour after seasoning

Nutritional Information Per Serving:

Calories 502 | Fat 25g |Sodium 230mg | Carbs 1.5g | Fiber 0.2g | Sugar 0.4g | Protein 64.1g

Teriyaki Chicken Skewers

Prep Time: 15 minutes.

Cook Time: 16 minutes.

Serves: 4

Ingredients:

- 453.5g boneless chicken thighs, cubed
- 237ml teriyaki marinade
- 16 small wooden skewers
- Sesame seeds for rolling

Teriyaki Marinade

- ⅓ cup soy sauce
- 59ml chicken broth
- ½ orange, juiced
- 2 tablespoons brown sugar
- 1 teaspoon ginger, grated
- 1 clove garlic, grated

Preparation:

1. Blend teriyaki marinade ingredients in a blender.

2. Add chicken and its marinade to a Ziplock bag.

3. Seal this bag, shake it well and refrigerate for 30 minutes..

4. Thread the chicken on the wooden skewers.

5. Place these skewers in the air fryer basket.

6. Return the air fryer basket to the Ninja Max XL Air Fryer.

7. Choose the "Air Fry" mode at 350 degrees F and 16 minutes of cooking time.

8. Initiate cooking by pressing the START/STOP BUTTON.

9. Flip the skewers once cooked halfway through.

10. Garnish with sesame seeds.

11. Serve warm.

Serving Suggestion: Serve on top of a bed of rocket leaves

Variation Tip: Mix the chicken with lemon juice seasoning

Nutritional Information Per Serving:

Calories 456 | Fat 16.4g |Sodium 1321mg | Carbs 19.2g | Fiber 2.2g | Sugar 4.2g | Protein 55.2g

Greek Chicken Meatballs

Prep Time: 10 minutes.

Cook Time: 9 minutes.

Serves: 4

Ingredients:

- 453.5g ground chicken
- 1 large egg
- 1½ tablespoon garlic paste
- 1 tablespoon dried oregano
- 1 teaspoon lemon zest
- 1 teaspoon dried onion powder
- ¾ teaspoon salt
- ¼ teaspoon black pepper
- Oil spray

Preparation:

1. Mix ground chicken with rest of the ingredients in a suitable bowl.
2. Make 1-inch sized meatballs out of this mixture.
3. Place the meatballs in the air fryer basket.
4. Return the air fryer basket to the Ninja Max XL Air Fryer.
5. Choose the "Air Fry" mode and set the temperature to 390 degrees F and 9 minutes of cooking time.
6. Initiate cooking by pressing the START/STOP BUTTON.
7. Serve warm.

Serving Suggestion: Serve with marinara sauce and pasta

Variation Tip: Coat the meatballs with breadcrumbs before cooking

Nutritional Information Per Serving:

Calories 346 | Fat 16.1g |Sodium 882mg | Carbs 1.3g | Fiber 0.5g | Sugar 0.5g | Protein 48.2g

Juicy Duck Breast

Prep Time: 10 minutes.

Cook Time: 20 minutes.

Serves: 1

Ingredients:

- ½ duck breast
- Salt and black pepper, to taste
- 2 tablespoons plum sauce

Preparation:

1. Rub the duck breast with black pepper and salt.
2. Place the duck breast in air fryer basket and add plum sauce on top.
3. Return the basket to the Ninja Max XL Air Fryer.
4. Choose the "Air Fry" mode and set the temperature to 400 degrees F and 20 minutes of cooking time.
5. Initiate cooking by pressing the START/STOP BUTTON.
6. Flip the duck breast once cooked halfway through.
7. Serve warm.

Serving Suggestion: Serve with tomato salad on the side

Variation Tip: Use poultry seasoning for breading

Nutritional Information Per Serving:

Calories 379 | Fat 19g |Sodium 184mg | Carbs 12.3g | Fiber 0.6g | Sugar 2g | Protein 37.7g

Bacon Wrapped Pork Tenderloin

Prep Time: 15 minutes.

Cook Time: 20 minutes.

Serves: 2

Ingredients:

- ½ teaspoons salt
- ¼ teaspoon black pepper
- 1 pork tenderloin
- 6 center cut strips bacon
- cooking string

Preparation:

1. Cut two bacon strips in half and place them on the working surface.

2. Place the other bacon strips on top and lay the tenderloin over the bacon strip.

3. Wrap the bacon around the tenderloin and tie the roast with a kitchen string.

4. Place the roast in the first air fryer basket.

5. Return the air fryer basket to the Ninja Max XL Air Fryer.

6. Choose the "Max Crisp" mode and set the temperature to 400 degrees F and 20 minutes of cooking time.

7. Initiate cooking by pressing the START/STOP BUTTON.

8. Slice and serve warm.

Serving Suggestion: Serve with sautéed green beans and cherry tomatoes

Variation Tip: Use honey glaze to baste the wrapped tenderloins

Nutritional Information Per Serving:

Calories 459 | Fat 17.7g |Sodium 1516mg | Carbs 1.7g | Fiber 0.5g | Sugar 0.4g | Protein 69.2g

Asian Pork Skewers

Prep Time: 10 minutes.

Cook Time: 25 minutes.

Serves: 4

Ingredients:

- 450g pork shoulder, sliced
- 30g ginger, peeled and crushed
- ½ tablespoons crushed garlic
- 67½ ml soy sauce
- 22½ ml honey
- 22½ ml rice vinegar
- 10ml toasted sesame oil
- 8 skewers

Preparation:

1. Pound the pork slices with a mallet.
2. Mix ginger, garlic, soy sauce, honey, rice vinegar, and sesame oil in a suitable bowl.
3. Add the prepared pork slices to the marinade and mix well to coat.
4. Cover and marinate the pork for 30 minutes..
5. Thread the pork on the wooden skewers and place them in the air fryer basket.
6. Return the air fryer basket to the Ninja Max XL Air Fryer.
7. Choose the "Air Fry" mode and set the temperature to 350 degrees F and 25 minutes of cooking time.
8. Initiate cooking by pressing the START/STOP BUTTON.
9. Flip the skewers once cooked halfway through.
10. Serve warm.

Serving Suggestion: Serve skewers with sautéed leeks or cabbages

Variation Tip: Mix the pork with lemon juice before seasoning

Nutritional Information Per Serving:

Calories 400 | Fat 32g |Sodium 721mg | Carbs 2.6g | Fiber 0g | Sugar 0g | Protein 27.4g

Steak and Asparagus Bundles

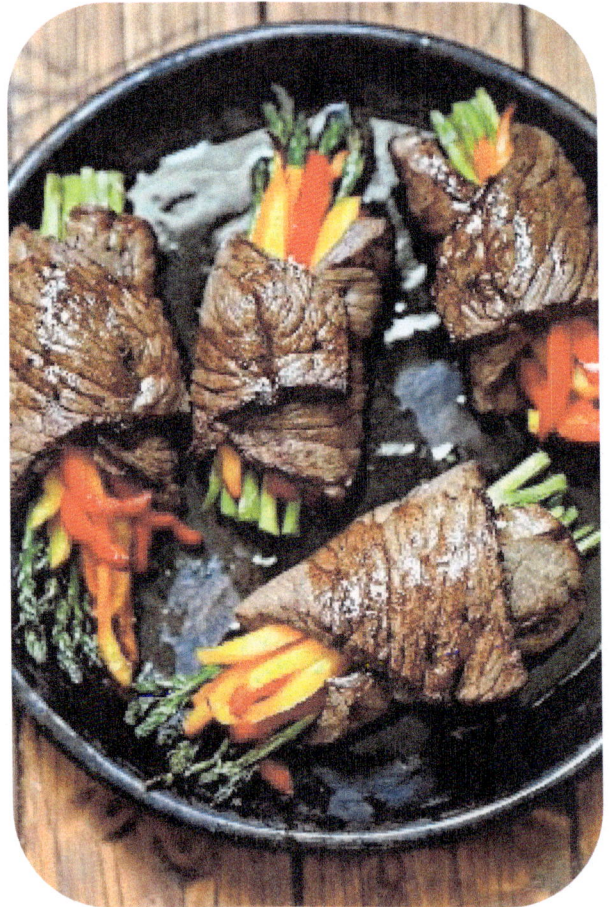

Prep Time: 15 minutes.

Cook Time: 10 minutes.

Serves: 6

Ingredients:

- 907g flank steak, cut into 6 pieces
- Salt and black pepper, to taste
- ½ cup tamari sauce

- 2 cloves garlic, crushed
- 1 pound asparagus, trimmed
- 3 capsicums, sliced
- ¼ cup balsamic vinegar
- 79 ml beef broth
- 2 tablespoons unsalted butter
- Olive oil spray

Preparation:

1. Mix steaks with black pepper, tamari sauce, and garlic in a Ziplock bag.
2. Seal this bag, shake well and refrigerate for 1 hour.
3. Place the steaks on the working surface and top each with asparagus and capsicums.
4. Roll the steaks and secure them with toothpicks.
5. Place these rolls in the air fryer basket.
6. Return the air fryer basket to the Ninja Max XL Air Fryer.
7. Choose the "Air Fry" mode and set the temperature to 400 degrees F and 10 minutes of cooking time.
8. Initiate cooking by pressing the START/STOP BUTTON.
9. Meanwhile, cook broth with butter and vinegar in a saucepan.
10. Cook this mixture until reduced by half and adjust seasoning with black pepper and salt.
11. Serve the steak rolls with the prepared sauce.

Serving Suggestion: Serve with fresh vegetable salad and marinara sauce

Variation Tip: Add freshly chopped parsley and coriander on top for a change of taste

Nutritional Information Per Serving:

Calories 551 | Fat 31g |Sodium 1329mg | Carbs 1.5g | Fiber 0.8g | Sugar 0.4g | Protein 64g

Beef Kabobs

Prep Time: 15 minutes.
Cook Time: 10 minutes.
Serves: 4

Ingredients:

- 1½ pounds sirloin steak, cut into 1-inch chunks
- 1 capsicum, diced
- 1 large red onion, diced

Marinade:

- 4 tablespoons olive oil
- 2 cloves garlic minced
- 1 tablespoon lemon juice
- ½ teaspoons
- ½ teaspoons
- Salt and black pepper, to taste

Preparation:

1. Mix beef with garlic, lemon juice and the rest of the ingredients in a suitable bowl.

2. Cover and refrigerate the beef for 30 minutes. for marination.

3. Place the skewers in the air fryer basket.

4. Return the air fryer basket to the Ninja Max XL Air Fryer.

5. Choose the "Air Fry" mode and set the temperature to 400 degrees F and 10 minutes of cooking time.

6. Initiate cooking by pressing the START/STOP BUTTON.

7. Flip the skewers once cooked halfway through.

8. Serve warm.

Serving Suggestion: Serve with Greek salad and crispy bread

Variation Tip: Mix the beef with lemon juice before seasoning

Nutritional Information Per Serving:

Calories 336 | Fat 27.1g |Sodium 66mg | Carbs 1.1g | Fiber 0.4g | Sugar 0.2g | Protein 19.7g

Air Fried Lamb Chops

Prep Time: 10 minutes.

Cook Time: 10 minutes.

Serves: 4

Ingredients:

- 700g lamb chops
- ½ teaspoon oregano
- 3 tablespoons parsley, minced
- ½ teaspoon black pepper
- 3 cloves garlic minced
- 2 tablespoons lemon juice
- 2 tablespoons olive oil
- Salt to taste

Preparation:

1. Pat dry the chops and mix with lemon juice and the rest of the ingredients.

2. Place these prepared chops in the air fryer basket.

3. Return the air fryer basket to the Ninja Max XL Air Fryer.

4. Choose the "Air Fry" mode and set the temperature to 400 degrees F and 10 minutes of cooking time.

5. Initiate cooking by pressing the START/STOP BUTTON.

6. Flip the pork chops once cooked halfway through.

7. Serve warm.

Serving Suggestion: Serve with boiled rice or steamed cauliflower rice

Variation Tip: Rub the chops with garlic cloves before seasoning

Nutritional Information Per Serving:

Calories 396 | Fat 23.2g |Sodium 622mg | Carbs 0.7g | Fiber 0g | Sugar 0g | Protein 45.6g

Cheesesteak Taquitos

Prep Time: 15 minutes.

Cook Time: 12 minutes.

Serves: 8

Ingredients:

- 1 pack soft corn tortillas
- 136g beef steak strips
- 2 green peppers, sliced
- 1 white onion, chopped
- 1 pkg dry Italian dressing mix
- 10 slices Provolone cheese
- Cooking spray or olive oil

Preparation:

1. Mix beef with cooking oil, peppers, onion, and dressing mix in a suitable bowl.

2. Add the strips in the air fryer basket.

3. Return the air fryer basket to the Ninja Max XL Air Fryer.

4. Choose the "Air Fry" mode at 375 degrees F and 12 minutes of cooking time.

5. Initiate cooking by pressing the START/STOP BUTTON.

6. Flip the strips once cooked halfway through.

7. Add the beef strips in the tortillas and top the beef with a beef slice.

8. Roll the tortillas and serve.

Serving Suggestion: Serve with roasted peppers and crouton salad

Variation Tip: Add shredded mozzarella cheese as well

Nutritional Information Per Serving:

Calories 410 | Fat 17.8g |Sodium 619mg | Carbs 21g | Fiber 1.4g | Sugar 1.8g | Protein 38.4g

Beef Kofta Kebab

Prep Time: 10 minutes.

Cook Time: 18 minutes.

Serves: 4

Ingredients:

- 1 pound ground beef
- ¼ cup white onion, grated
- ¼ cup parsley, chopped
- 1 tablespoon mint, chopped
- 2 cloves garlic, minced
- 1 teaspoon salt
- ½ teaspoons cumin
- 1 teaspoon oregano
- ½ teaspoons garlic salt
- 1 egg

Preparation:

1. Mix ground beef with onion, parsley, mint, garlic, cumin, oregano, garlic salt and egg in a suitable bowl.

2. Take 3 tbsp-sized beef kebabs out of this mixture.

3. Place the kebabs in the air fryer basket.

4. Return the air fryer basket to the Ninja Max XL Air Fryer.

5. Choose the "Air Fry" mode at 375 degrees F and 18 minutes of cooking time.

6. Initiate cooking by pressing the START/STOP BUTTON.

7. Flip the kebabs once cooked halfway through.

8. Serve warm.

Serving Suggestion: Serve with avocado or yogurt dip

Variation Tip: Coat with breadcrumbs before cooking for a crispy texture

Nutritional Information Per Serving:

Calories 316 | Fat 12.2g |Sodium 587mg | Carbs 12.2g | Fiber 1g | Sugar 1.8g | Protein 25.8g

BBQ Pork Chops

Prep Time: 15 minutes.

Cook Time: 12 minutes.

Serves: 4

Ingredients:

- 4 pork chops
- Salt and black pepper to taste
- 1 package BBQ Shake & Bake
- Olive oil

Preparation:

1. Season pork chops with black pepper, salt, BBQ shake and olive oil.

2. Place these prepared chops in the air fryer basket.

3. Return the air fryer basket to the Ninja Max XL Air Fryer.

4. Choose the "Air Fry" mode at 375 degrees F and 12 minutes of cooking time.

5. Initiate cooking by pressing the START/STOP BUTTON.

6. Flip the pork chops once cooked halfway through.

7. Serve warm.

Serving Suggestion: Serve with tomato ketchup or chili sauce

Variation Tip: Coat chops with breadcrumbs for a crispy texture

Nutritional Information Per Serving:
Calories 437 | Fat 28g |Sodium 1221mg | Carbs 22.3g | Fiber 0.9g | Sugar 8g | Protein 30.3g

Cinnamon-Apple Pork Chops

Prep Time: 15 minutes.

Cook Time: 10 minutes.

Serves: 4

Ingredients:

- 2 tablespoons butter
- 4 boneless pork loin chops
- 3 tablespoons brown sugar
- 1 teaspoon ground cinnamon
- ½ teaspoons ground nutmeg
- ¼ teaspoon salt
- 4 medium tart apples, sliced
- 2 tablespoons chopped pecans

Preparation:

1. Mix butter, brown sugar, cinnamon, nutmeg, and salt in a suitable bowl.
2. Rub this mixture over the pork chops and place them in the air fryer basket.
3. Top them with apples and pecans.
4. Return the air fryer basket to the Ninja Max XL Air Fryer.
5. Choose the "Air Fry" mode at 375 degrees F and 10 minutes of cooking time.
6. Initiate cooking by pressing the START/STOP BUTTON.
7. Serve warm.

Serving Suggestion: Serve with sauteed broccoli florets

Variation Tip: Add chopped almonds or walnuts instead of pecans

Nutritional Information Per Serving:
Calories 316 | Fat 17g |Sodium 271mg | Carbs 4.3g | Fiber 0.9g | Sugar 2.1g | Protein 35g

Pork Chops and Potatoes

Prep Time: 15 minutes.

Cook Time: 12 minutes.

Serves: 3

Ingredients:

- 453.5g red potatoes
- Olive oil
- Salt and pepper
- 1 teaspoon garlic powder
- 1 teaspoon fresh rosemary, chopped
- 2 tablespoons brown sugar
- 1 tablespoon soy sauce
- 1 tablespoon Worcestershire sauce
- 1 teaspoon lemon juice
- 3 small pork chops

Preparation:

1. Mix potatoes and pork chops with remaining ingredients in a suitable bowl.
2. Add the ingredients in the air fryer basket.
3. Return the air fryer basket to the Ninja Max XL Air Fryer.
4. Choose the "Air Fry" mode at 400 degrees F and 12 minutes of cooking time.
5. Initiate cooking by pressing the START/STOP BUTTON.
6. Flip the chops and toss potatoes once cooked halfway through.
7. Serve warm.

Serving Suggestion: Serve with sautéed courgetti and green beans

Variation Tip: Rub the pork chops with lemon juice before seasoning

Nutritional Information Per Serving:

Calories 352 | Fat 9.1g |Sodium 1294mg |

Carbs 3.9g | Fiber 1g | Sugar 1g | Protein 61g

Pork Chops with Apples

Prep Time: 20 minutes.

Cook Time: 15 minutes.

Serves: 2

Ingredients:

- ½ small red cabbage, sliced
- 1 apple, sliced
- 1 sweet onion, sliced
- 2 tablespoons oil
- ½ teaspoons cumin
- ½ teaspoons paprika
- Salt and black pepper, to taste
- 2 boneless pork chops (1" thick)

Preparation:

1. Toss pork chops with apple and the rest of the ingredients in a suitable bowl.
2. Add the mixture in the air fryer basket.

3. Return the air fryer basket to the Ninja Max XL Air Fryer.

4. Choose the "Air Fry" mode and set the temperature to 400 degrees F and 15 minutes of cooking time.

5. Initiate cooking by pressing the START/STOP BUTTON.

6. Serve warm.

Serving Suggestion: Serve on top of boiled white rice

Variation Tip: Add Worcestershire sauce and honey to taste

Nutritional Information Per Serving:
Calories 374 | Fat 25g |Sodium 275mg | Carbs 7.3g | Fiber 0g | Sugar 6g | Protein 12.3g

Steak Bites with Cowboy Butter

Prep Time: 15 minutes.
Cook Time: 15 minutes.
Serves: 4

Ingredients:

- 453.5g steak sirloin
- Cooking spray

Cowboy butter sauce

- 1 stick salted butter melted
- 1 tablespoon lemon zest
- 1 tablespoon lemon juice
- ½ teaspoon garlic powder
- ¼ teaspoon red pepper flakes
- ½ teaspoon sea salt
- ½ teaspoon black pepper
- ½ tablespoon Dijon mustard
- ½ teaspoon Worcestershire sauce
- 1 tablespoon parsley freshly chopped

Preparation:

1. Mix all the cowboy butter ingredients in a suitable bowl.
2. Stir in steak cubes and mix well.
3. Then cover and marinate them in the refrigerator for 1 hour.
4. Add the steak cubes in the air fryer basket then use cooking spray.
5. Return the air fryer basket to the Ninja Max XL Air Fryer.
6. Choose the "Air Fry" mode at 400 degrees F and 15 minutes of cooking time.
7. Initiate cooking by pressing the START/STOP BUTTON.
8. Serve warm.

Serving Suggestion: Serve the steak bites with flatbread

Variation Tip: Add a drizzle of lemon juice before serving

Nutritional Information Per Serving:
Calories 264 | Fat 17g |Sodium 129mg | Carbs 0.9g | Fiber 0.3g | Sugar 0g | Protein 27g

Dessert Recipes

Baked Apples

Prep Time: 10 minutes.

Cook Time: 15 minutes.

Serves: 4

Ingredients:

- 4 apples
- 6 teaspoons raisins
- 2 teaspoons chopped walnuts
- 2 teaspoons honey
- ½ teaspoon cinnamon

Preparation:

1. Chop off the head of the apples and scoop out the flesh from the center.

2. Stuff the apples with raisins, walnuts, honey and cinnamon.

3. Place these apples in the air fryer basket.

4. Return the air fryer basket of the Ninja Max XL Air Fryer.

5. Choose the "Air Fry" mode and set the temperature to 350 degrees F and 15 minutes of cooking time.

6. Initiate cooking by pressing the START/STOP BUTTON.

7. Serve.

Serving Suggestion: Serve the apples cup of spice latte or hot chocolate

Variation Tip: Top the apples with melted chocolate for a change of taste

Nutritional Information Per Serving:

Calories 175 | Fat 13.1g |Sodium 154mg | Carbs 14g | Fiber 0.8g | Sugar 8.9g | Protein 0.7g

Cinnamon Bread Twists

Prep Time: 15 minutes.

Cook Time: 15 minutes.

Serves: 4

Ingredients:

Bread Twists Dough

- 120g all-purpose flour
- 1 teaspoon baking powder
- ¼ teaspoon salt
- 150g fat free Greek yogurt

Brushing

- 2 tablespoons light butter
- 2 tablespoons granulated sugar
- 1-2 teaspoons ground cinnamon, to taste

Preparation:

1. Mix 120g flour, salt and baking powder in a suitable bowl.
2. Stir in yogurt and the rest of the dough ingredients in a suitable bowl.
3. Mix well and make 8 inches long strips out of this dough.
4. Twist the strips and place them in the air fryer basket.
5. Return the air fryer basket to the Ninja Max XL Air Fryer.
6. Choose the "Air Fry" mode at 375 degrees F and 15 minutes of cooking time.
7. Initiate cooking by pressing the START/STOP BUTTON.
8. Flip the twists once cooked halfway through.
9. Mix butter with cinnamon and sugar in a suitable bowl.
10. Brush this mixture over the twists.
11. Serve.

Serving Suggestion: Serve with butter pecan ice cream or strawberry jam

Variation Tip: Add maple syrup on top

Nutritional Information Per Serving:

Calories 391 | Fat 24g |Sodium 142mg | Carbs 38.5g | Fiber 3.5g | Sugar 21g | Protein 6.6g

Bread Pudding

Prep Time: 10 minutes.

Cook Time: 15 minutes.

Serves: 4

Ingredients:

- 2 cups bread cubes
- 1 egg
- ⅔ cup heavy cream
- ½ teaspoons vanilla extract
- ¼ cup sugar
- ¼ cup chocolate chips

Preparation:

1. Grease an 8 inches baking dish with a cooking spray.

2. Add the bread cubes in the baking dish and sprinkle chocolate chips on top.

3. Beat egg with cream, sugar and vanilla in a suitable bowl.

4. Add this mixture to the baking pan.

5. Place the pan in the air fryer basket.

6. Return the air fryer basket to the Ninja Max XL Air Fryer.

7. Choose the "Air Fry" mode at 350 degrees F and 15 minutes of cooking time.

8. Initiate cooking by pressing the START/STOP BUTTON.

9. Allow the pudding to cool and serve.

Serving Suggestion: Serve with a dollop of vanilla ice-cream on top

Variation Tip: Drizzle chopped nuts on top

Nutritional Information Per Serving:

Calories 149 | Fat 1.2g |Sodium 3mg | Carbs 37.6g | Fiber 5.8g | Sugar 29g | Protein 1.1g

Grilled Peaches

Prep Time: 10 minutes.

Cook Time: 5 minutes.

Serves: 2

Ingredients:

- 2 yellow peaches, peeled and cut into wedges
- ¼ cup graham cracker crumbs
- ¼ cup brown sugar
- ¼ cup butter diced into tiny cubes
- Whipped cream or ice cream

Preparation:

1. Toss peaches with crumbs, brown sugar, and butter in a suitable bowl.

2. Spread the peaches in one air fryer basket.

3. Return the air fryer basket to the Ninja Max XL Air Fryer.

4. Choose the "Air Fry" mode and set the temperature to 350 degrees F and 5 minutes of cooking time.

5. Initiate cooking by pressing the START/STOP BUTTON.

6. Serve the prepared peaches with a scoop of ice cream.

Serving Suggestion: Serve with a dollop of sweet cream dip

Variation Tip: Add chopped raisins and nuts on top of the peaches

Nutritional Information Per Serving:

Calories 327 | Fat 14.2g |Sodium 672mg | Carbs 47.2g | Fiber 1.7g | Sugar 24.8g | Protein 4.

Dessert Empanadas

Prep Time: 10 minutes.

Cook Time: 10 minutes.

Serves: 12

Ingredients:

- 12 empanada wrappers thawed
- 2 apples, chopped
- 2 tablespoons raw honey
- 1 teaspoon vanilla extract
- 1 teaspoon cinnamon
- ⅛ teaspoon nutmeg
- 2 teaspoons cornstarch
- 1 teaspoon water
- 1 egg beaten

Preparation:

1. Mix apples with vanilla, honey, nutmeg, and cinnamon in a saucepan.

2. Cook for 3 minutes. then mix cornstarch with water and pour into the pan.

3. Cook for 30 seconds.

4. Allow this filling to cool and keep it aside.

5. Spread the wrappers on the working surface.

6. Add the apple filling on top of the wrappers.

7. Fold the wrappers in half and seal the edges by pressing them.

8. Brush the prepared empanadas with the beaten egg and place them in the air fryer basket.

9. Return the air fryer basket of the Ninja Max XL Air Fryer.

10. Choose the "Air Fry" mode at 400 degrees F and 10 minutes of cooking time.

11. Initiate cooking by pressing the START/STOP BUTTON.

12. Flip the empanadas once cooked halfway through.

13. Serve.

Serving Suggestion: Serve with cranberry jam on the side

Variation Tip: Add raisins or dried cranberries to the filling

Nutritional Information Per Serving:

Calories 204 | Fat 9g |Sodium 91mg | Carbs 27g | Fiber 2.4g | Sugar 15g | Protein 1.3g

Monkey Bread

Prep Time: 15 minutes.

Cook Time: 10 minutes.

Serves: 12

Ingredients:

Bread

- 12 Rhodes white dinner rolls
- ½ cup brown sugar
- 1 teaspoon cinnamon
- 4 tablespoons butter melted

Glaze

- ½ cup powdered sugar
- 1-2 tablespoons milk
- ½ teaspoon vanilla

Preparation:

1. Mix ½ cup brown sugar, cinnamon and butter in a suitable bowl.
2. Cut the dinner rolls in half and dip them in the sugar mixture.
3. Place these buns in a greased baking pan and pour the remaining butter on top.
4. Place the buns in the air fryer basket.
5. Return the air fryer basket to the Ninja Max XL Air Fryer.
6. Choose the "Air Fry" mode at 350 degrees F and 10 minutes of cooking time.
7. Initiate cooking by pressing the START/STOP BUTTON.
8. Flip the rolls once cooked halfway through.
9. Meanwhile, mix milk, vanilla and sugar in a suitable bowl.
10. Pour the glaze over the air fried rolls.
11. Serve.

Serving Suggestion: Serve the bread with chocolate syrup on top

Variation Tip: Add honey to the butter glaze

Nutritional Information Per Serving:

Calories 192 | Fat 9.3g |Sodium 133mg |
Carbs 27.1g | Fiber 1.4g | Sugar 19g | Protein 3.2g

Strawberry Shortcake

Prep Time: 10 minutes.
Cook Time: 9 minutes.
Serves: 8

Ingredients:

Strawberry topping

- 1-pint strawberries sliced
- ½ cup confectioner's sugar substitute

Shortcake

- 2 cups Carbquick baking biscuit mix
- ¼ cup butter cold, cubed
- ½ cup confectioner's sugar substitute
- Pinch salt
- ⅔ cup water
- Garnish: sugar free whipped cream

Preparation:

1. Mix the shortcake ingredients in a suitable bowl until smooth.

2. Add the dough into 6 biscuits.

3. Place the biscuits in the air fryer basket.

4. Return the air fryer basket of the Ninja Max XL Air Fryer.

5. Choose the "Air Fry" mode and set the temperature 400 degrees F and 9 minutes of cooking time.

6. Initiate cooking by pressing the START/STOP BUTTON.

7. Mix strawberries with sugar in a saucepan and cook until the mixture thickens.

8. Slice the biscuits in half and add strawberry sauce in between two halves of a biscuit.

9. Serve.

Serving Suggestion: Serve with maple syrup on top

Variation Tip: Add orange juice and zest to the cake for change of taste

Nutritional Information Per Serving:
Calories 157 | Fat 1.3g |Sodium 27mg | Carbs 1.3g | Fiber 1g | Sugar 2.2g | Protein 8.2g

Blueberry Pie Egg Rolls

Prep Time: 10 minutes.

Cook Time: 5 minutes.

Serves: 12

Ingredients:

- 12 egg roll wrappers
- 2 cups of blueberries
- 1 tablespoon of cornstarch
- ½ cup of agave nectar
- 1 teaspoon of lemon zest
- 2 tablespoons of water
- 1 tablespoon of lemon juice
- Olive oil or butter flavored cooking spray
- Confectioner's sugar for dusting

Preparation:

1. Mix blueberries with cornstarch, lemon zest, agave and water in a saucepan.

2. Cook this mixture for 5 minutes. on a simmer.

3. Allow the mixture to cool.

4. Spread the roll wrappers and Add the filling at the center of the wrappers.

5. Fold the two edges and roll each wrapper.

6. Wet and seal the wrappers then place them in the air fryer basket.

7. Spray these rolls with cooking spray.

8. Return the air fryer basket of the Ninja Max XL Air Fryer.

9. Choose the "Air Fry" mode at 350 degrees F temperature and 5 minutes of cooking time.

10. Initiate cooking by pressing the START/STOP BUTTON.

11. Dust the rolls with confectioner' sugar.

12. Serve.

Serving Suggestion: Serve the rolls with a warming cup of hot chocolate

Variation Tip: Use raspberries or strawberry filling instead of blueberry filling for change of taste

Nutritional Information Per Serving:

Calories 258 | Fat 12.4g |Sodium 79mg | Carbs 34.3g | Fiber 1g | Sugar 17g | Protein 3.2g

Victoria Sponge Cake

Prep Time: 15 minutes.
Cook Time: 16 minutes.
Serves: 8

Ingredients:

Sponge Cake Ingredients

- 400g self-rising flour
- 450g caster sugar
- 50g lemon curd
- 200g butter
- 4 medium eggs
- 1 tablespoon vanilla essence
- 480ml skimmed milk
- 1 tablespoon olive oil
- 4 tablespoon strawberry jam

Strawberry buttercream

- 115g butter
- 210g icing sugar
- ½ teaspoon strawberry food coloring
- 1 tablespoon single cream
- 1 teaspoon vanilla essence
- 1 teaspoon maple syrup

Preparation:

1. Mix sugar and butter in a suitable bowl using a hand mixer.
2. Beat eggs with oil, and vanilla in a suitable bowl with the mixer until creamy.
3. Stir in milk, flour and curd then mix well.
4. Add butter mixture then mix well.
5. Divide this mixture in two 4 inches greased cake pans.
6. Place one pan in the air fryer basket at a time.
7. Return the air fryer basket to the Ninja Max XL Air Fryer.
8. Choose the "Air Fry" mode and set the temperature to 375 degrees F and 16 minutes of cooking time.
9. Initiate cooking by pressing the START/STOP BUTTON.
10. Cook the remaining batter in the pan in the same way.
11. Meanwhile, blend the buttercream ingredients in a mixer until fluffy.
12. Then place a cake on a plate and top it with the buttercream.
13. Top it jam and then with the other cake.
14. Serve.

Serving Suggestion: Serve with a cup of hot coffee

Variation Tip: Add shredded nuts and coconuts to the filling

Nutritional Information Per Serving:
Calories 284 | Fat 16g |Sodium 252mg | Carbs 31.6g | Fiber 0.9g | Sugar 6.6g | Protein 3.7g

Week 1

Monday:

Breakfast: Brussels Sprouts Potato Hash

Lunch: Honey Teriyaki Salmon

Snack: Bacon Wrapped Tater Tot

Dinner: Thai Curry Chicken Kabobs

Dessert: Bread Pudding

Tuesday

Breakfast: Cheesy Baked Eggs

Lunch: Cajun Scallops

Snack: Crispy Popcorn Shrimp

Dinner: Greek Chicken Meatballs

Dessert: Baked Apples

Wednesday

Breakfast: Sausage Breakfast Casserole

Lunch: Furikake Salmon

Snack: Avocado Fries with Sriracha Dip

Dinner: Chicken Caprese

Dessert: Blueberry Pie Egg Rolls

Thursday

Breakfast: Roasted Oranges

Lunch: Tuna Steaks

Snack: Onion Rings

Dinner: Cornish Hen

Dessert: Strawberry Shortcake

Friday

Breakfast: Breakfast Frittata

Lunch: Shrimp with Lemon and Pepper

Snack: Potato Chips

Dinner: Teriyaki Chicken Skewers

Dessert: Dessert Empanadas

Saturday

Breakfast: Jelly Doughnuts

Lunch: Stuffed Mushrooms with Crab

Snack: Crab Cakes

Dinner: Chicken Kebabs

Dessert: Monkey Bread

Sunday

Breakfast: Apple Fritters

Lunch: Foil Packet Salmon

Snack: Fried Ravioli

Dinner: Juicy Duck Breast

Dessert: Grilled Peaches

Week 2

Monday:

Breakfast: Breakfast Stuffed Peppers

Lunch: Air Fryer Calamari

Snack: Fried Cheese

Dinner: Crispy Fried Quail

Dessert: Bread Pudding

Tuesday

Breakfast: Breakfast Potatoes

Lunch: Honey Pecan Shrimp

Snack: Cinnamon Sugar Chickpeas

Dinner: Asian Pork Skewers

Dessert: Cinnamon Bread Twists

Wednesday

Breakfast: Cornbread

Lunch: Crumb-Topped Sole

Snack: Onion Rings

Dinner: Beef Kofta Kebab

Dessert: Victoria Sponge Cake

Thursday

Breakfast: Brussels Sprouts Potato Hash

Lunch: Pretzel-Crusted Catfish

Snack: Bacon Wrapped Tater Tot

Dinner: Beef Kabobs

Dessert: Dessert Empanadas

Friday

Breakfast: Cheesy Baked Eggs

Lunch: Brown Sugar Garlic Salmon

Snack: Crispy Popcorn Shrimp

Dinner: Steak and Asparagus Bundles

Dessert: Blueberry Pie Egg Rolls

Saturday

Breakfast: Sausage Breakfast Casserole

Lunch: Chili Lime Tilapia

Snack: Avocado Fries with Sriracha Dip

Dinner: Cheesesteak Taquitos

Dessert: Baked Apples

Sunday

Breakfast: Roasted Oranges

Lunch: Crispy Parmesan Cod

Snack: Onion Rings

Dinner: Air Fried Lamb Chops

Dessert: Blueberry Pie Egg Rolls

Week 3

Monday:

Breakfast: Breakfast Frittata

Lunch: Bacon Wrapped Stuffed Chicken

Snack: Potato Chips

Dinner: BBQ Pork Chops

Dessert: Strawberry Shortcake

Tuesday

Breakfast: Jelly Doughnuts

Lunch: Pretzel Chicken Cordon Bleu

Snack: Crab Cakes

Dinner: Pork Chops with Apples

Dessert: Dessert Empanadas

Wednesday

Breakfast: Apple Fritters

Lunch: Chicken and Potatoes

Snack: Fried Ravioli

Dinner: Cinnamon-Apple Pork Chops

Dessert: Monkey Bread

Thursday

Breakfast: Breakfast Stuffed Peppers

Lunch: Crispy Sesame Chicken

Snack: Fried Cheese

Dinner: Bacon Wrapped Pork Tenderloin

Dessert: Grilled Peaches

Friday

Breakfast: Breakfast Potatoes

Lunch: Jamaican Fried Chicken

Snack: Cinnamon Sugar Chickpeas

Dinner: Steak Bites with Cowboy Butter

Dessert: Cinnamon Bread Twists

Saturday

Breakfast: Cornbread

Lunch: Air Fried Chicken Legs

Snack: Bacon Wrapped Tater Tot

Dinner: Air Fried Lamb Chops

Dessert: Victoria Sponge Cake

Sunday

Breakfast: Roasted Oranges

Lunch: Crispy Parmesan Cod

Snack: Onion Rings

Dinner: Air Fried Lamb Chops

Dessert: Blueberry Pie Egg Rolls

Week 4

Monday:

Breakfast: Brussels Sprouts Potato Hash

Lunch: Honey Teriyaki Salmon

Snack: Bacon Wrapped Tater Tot

Dinner: Thai Curry Chicken Kabobs

Dessert: Bread Pudding

Tuesday

Breakfast: Cheesy Baked Eggs

Lunch: Cajun Scallops

Snack: Crispy Popcorn Shrimp

Dinner: Greek Chicken Meatballs

Dessert: Baked Apples

Wednesday

Breakfast: Sausage Breakfast Casserole

Lunch: Furikake Salmon

Snack: Avocado Fries with Sriracha Dip

Dinner: Chicken Caprese

Dessert: Blueberry Pie Egg Rolls

Thursday

Breakfast: Roasted Oranges

Lunch: Tuna Steaks

Snack: Onion Rings

Dinner: Cornish Hen

Dessert: Strawberry Shortcake

Friday

Breakfast: Breakfast Frittata

Lunch: Shrimp with Lemon and Pepper

Snack: Potato Chips

Dinner: Teriyaki Chicken Skewers

Dessert: Dessert Empanadas

Saturday

Breakfast: Jelly Doughnuts

Lunch: Stuffed Mushrooms with Crab

Snack: Crab Cakes

Dinner: Chicken Kebabs

Dessert: Monkey Bread

Sunday

Breakfast: Apple Fritters

Lunch: Foil Packet Salmon

Snack: Fried Ravioli

Dinner: Juicy Duck Breast

Dessert: Grilled Peaches

Conclusion

Aren't you going to try the MAX crispy recipes in this cookbook with the Ninja Max XL Air Fryer? Well, here is your chance to do so, right away! The Ninja Max XL Air Fryer is a convenient and quick way to prepare your favorite foods. In a family-sized 5.5-quart basket, cook and crisp 3 pounds of French fries with little to no oil. Maxcrisp technology uses 450°F superheated air to cook dishes up to 30 percent faster, resulting in hotter, crispier results with little to no oil for guilt-free fried favorites. So, let's get started with this cookbook!

Printed in Great Britain
by Amazon